We Who Would Take no Prisoners: Selections From the Fifth International Conference on Penal Abolition

Edited by
Brian D. MacLean
Harold E. Pepinsky

Collective Press
Vancouver

© Collective Press 1993
Vancouver
Printed in Canada

ISBN 0-9694764-3-4

Canadian Cataloguing in Publication Data

Main entry under title:

We who would take no prisoners: selections from the fifth
international conference on penal abolition

ISBN 0-9694764-3-4 (pbk.)

1. Criminology. 2. Corrections. 3. Penology
I. MacLean, Brian D., 1950-
II. Pepinsky, Harold E., 1945-

128 pp

Cover photo courtesy of *Regina Leader Post*

for all those involved in the struggle for penal abolition

Contents

Preface

We are among the pacifists of criminal justice. International Conferences on Penal Abolition (ICOPA) are not an organization; all we do is pass the conference from one set of hands to another. ICOPA conferences are a channel through which those who dare to explore options for punishing criminals extend their awareness of one another. When there seems so little place for our views in public opinion as media portrayed, in the texts we teach from, or in our scholarly journals, ICOPA helps to provide that space. Every ICOPA extends the personal knowledge of its participants. The knowledge they impart (as, for example, through this volume) is that penal abolition is a pervasive, active, innovative force inside prison and out, worldwide.

ICOPA V was held in Bloomington, Indiana. The first of these biennial conferences to be held in the United States – May 22–25, 1991, ICOPA V was sponsored by the Department of Criminal Justice at Indiana University. A total of 150 registered participants were hosted from as far east as St. Petersburg; as far south as San Jose, Costa Rica; as far west as the eastern Pacific rim; and a large contingent of steadfast Native and Canadian abolitionists attended from the north. As many as half of our participants were subsidized by individual private donations to help focus our attention on the criminal justice plight of peoples of color. These included a delegation from the National Interreligious Task Force on Criminal Justice, and a group of Native North Americans – elder, Art Solomon; spiritual advisers, OohwahNah Chasing Bear, and Lennie Foster; and a number of ex-prisoners actively supporting sisters and brothers in prison, notably in the struggle to worship in their traditional ways inside prison walls. Art opened and OohwahNah closed the conference with their prayers.

Previous ICOPA conferences have been held in Toronto, Amsterdam, Montreal, and Kazimierz Dolny, Poland. Two years after ICOPA V, ICOPA VI, hosted by Deputy Director, Elias Carranza, and his United Nations Latin American Institute for Crime Prevention and Treatment of Criminality, was held at the Justice Building in San Jose, Costa Rica, June 2-5, 1993. There were 200 participants, largely an imaginative and active new-to-us group of Latin Americans. We were also joined by a substantial group from New Zealand committed to organizing ICOPA conferences in that region. Elias Carranza plans to publish papers from ICOPA VI (contact him c/o ILANUD, Apartado 10071-1000, San Jose, COSTA RICA, for information).

ICOPA VII will be held late May 1995 in Barcelona, Spain (contact Teresa Sanchez Concheiro, Abogada, Barcelona, SPAIN C/Aragon 321.4*). This location was chosen by consensus in San Jose as has become customary at the closing town meeting of each ICOPA.

ICOPA has also become a channel for introducing our movement to new audiences. This volume is such an effort.

Chapter 1 introduces penal abolition as it is seen by those who are interested in talking with penal abolitionists but are not yet ready to fully endorse abolition. Jim Thomas has been involved in prison research and reform since 1980; Sharon Boehlefeld is a journalist; they collaborated on this essay while she was finishing her MA in the Department of Sociology, Northern Illinois University where Jim teaches. The book they review is the major publication inspired by ICOPA III in Montreal in 1987. Willem de Haan was active in the first three ICOPA conferences.

As in this volume, every ICOPA conference welcomes dialogue with skeptics who are not willing to give up on the idea that we might need prisons to be safe. We accept responsibility for trying to translate our faith in restorative justice into terms theoretically and practically acceptable to skeptics. But we who would take no prisoners have long since learned that the discourse of abolition goes beyond the categories into which skeptics would stereotype us and deny the totality of our arguments. Is Fay Honey Knopp merely a social critic/sociologist? She calls herself a Quaker feminist abolitionist. Her spiritual commitment drives her practical quest to invent and evaluate alternatives to prison; her approach – offering programmatic options to victims and offenders in sexual violence cases – is eminently worldly and honestly inquisitive. Is Mathiesen *the* progenitor of contemporary abolitionism, or is he not drawing on established traditions of thought and action (for example, he credits Mao Zedong for inspiring him to think of abolitionism as an unfinished revolution)? And when abolitionists speak with or to outsiders, as de Haan does in the book Thomas and Boehlefeld review, we all struggle as Willem does to find the magic word or concept that will be definitive for our readers. That definition of who we are remains elusive, and inherently ambiguous. We abolitionists allow ourselves to express what the term means and what we are doing about it in individual terms.

Chapter 1 represents the sympathetic dialogue we abolitionists seek with skeptics because, as Ari Hirvonen makes clear, there is strong consensus among us that dialogue has a restorative power of its own. Such dialogue creates an understanding of abolitionism precisely because we refuse to dictate the terms upon which the subject should be discussed. We recognize the truth in the opening sentence of chapter 1: 'Few people take prison abolitionists seriously ....

We face the reality that while we remain committed to extending our network of inquiry into the potential for penal abolition, we have no self-contained body of knowledge to represent fully in one volume. Hal Pepinsky began the editorial process for the selections that follow by boiling down about fifteen hours of transcripts from ICOPA V sessions and approximately twenty papers into a manuscript. Brian MacLean, who was not at ICOPA V, then took on the practical task of selecting about half that material to create an affordable volume that we could publish without another two-to-three-year delay. We have given up any pretense of reporting on the conference as a whole. Many people who have made major contributions at ICOPA V itself, let alone in and around ICOPA conferences over the years, are not named in this volume including Thomas and Boehlefeld's opening and Frank Dunbaugh's closing histories of previous ICOPA conferences. This volume should neither be treated as a *Who's Who* of ICOPA V nor of the penal abolition movement. Rather, we editors agree that this snapshot indicates both the depth and breadth of ICOPA V. This volume especially taps the depth of concern for the urgent tragedy of the US death penalty, and for the ubiquity of racism, a process in which people of color are mistreated – most revealingly in a quest to wipe out the Native worship of an abolitionist Creator. As well, we aim to convey the breadth of the cultural and occupational lives of penal abolitionists. Academic overviews and reflections are provided; African prisoner revolution is discussed; the importance of Native spiritual support for abolitionism, both for people inside and outside prison, is examined; ways to help heal the wounds of sexual violence are explored; and legal change, political lobbying, and education receive attention. At the same time, the chapters are but slices of the lives of their authors, all of whom cross roles as theorists, educators, and activists somehow working in the trenches of penal-law. The lives of abolitionists seem to preclude occupational and intellectual specialization.

Chapter 2 provides some remarks made by opponents of the death penalty in the United States, the only country in the world which has returned to the death penalty. This decision was not made on grounds of national emergency, but simply because judges changed their minds and said 'you can do it if you want to.' The US government fails to ratify the UN convention on the rights of children because they do not want to prevent states from executing offenders under eighteen. Execution is the only US criminal justice policy condemned as a human rights violation in itself by Amnesty International, a major international human rights organization with whom Clare Regan (chapter 2) works.

Death penalty lawyers are as highly organized and mobilized as any public interest law group in the United States. By appealing to the consciences of lower-level trial and appellate judges, they have placed many serious objections to the death penalty before the courts. Now, even when these lawyers introduce new evidence, available subsequent to trial, that clearly exonerates the death-row prisoner, the courts claim that the prisoner must die because 'it's too late, there are no excuses.' Thus the only reason to tolerate the death penalty is because we do not allow ourselves to accept any excuses for flimsy evidence. For example, as Clare Regan describes him, the only thing that death-row prisoner Willie Darden has in common with a murderer is that he was a Black man in the neighborhood. Delbert Tibbs of the National Interreligious Task Force and the National Coalition to Abolish the Death Penalty, Bob Gross of the National Coalition, and Clare attempt to force the US public to confront the reality of capital punishment. We must progress beyond the mindless susceptibility and the political exploitation of accepting the courts logic of 'no excuses' for stopping the death-penalty machine.

In chapter 3, former prisoners speak to us. Actually, they are still prisoners as they make clear. We will not have learned to (re)habilitate prisoners until we can accept the prisoners who return to us. Some prisoners are easily identified by their tattoos, with others it may take a job application to make you aware of what they remain – an 'ex-convict,' likely to recidivate, in a class apart from the rest. One of the few 'legitimate' avenues to supporting oneself available in the community to ex-prisoners is working in support of sisters and brothers who remain locked away. That is the path taken by ex-prisoners Tony Nieto, a Mescalero Apache; Lionel White Bird, a Plains Cree Indian; and African US citizen, Achebe Lateef.

Whatever corrupts our relations outside corrupts most absolutely in prisons, where, as Tony Nieto tells us, authorities refuse to accept evidence that a prisoner has been murdered. (It happens regularly, just ask the prisoners.) In the same way that our awareness of the realities of Willie Darden and Delbert Tibbs reinforces our opposition to the death penalty, our awareness of what prisoners know of prison conditions, and of the frustration and suppression of many attempts to give voice to prisoners, reinforces our opposition to imprisonment. What imprisonment does to the keepers, frightens us as well.

In chapter 4, Fay Honey Knopp discusses one of the earliest texts in abolitionism – her 1976 book, *Instead of Prisons*. As Ari Hirvonen indicates in chapter 7, radical feminism has come to occupy a major position in abolitionist thinking. In this context, a key premise of radical feminism is that domination itself is the source of social misery and injustice. The empowerment of people adversely affected by human conflict is the only way to promote healing from that conflict without compounding the violence and its attendant pain. For over fifty years, Honey Knopp has worked to prevent and redress sexual violence, perhaps today the most politically sensitive and explosive areas of popular concerns with 'criminality.' She at once explains what we might do instead of punishing our most repulsive offenders, and offers a more encompassing vision of what abolitionist justice entails. She represents a large group of abolitionists who place a high priority on confronting violence against women and children; nonetheless, they reject punishing offenders as impractical and immoral. Negative popular images of feminism often portray feminists as demanding criminal justice solutions to the social problem of gender inequity. Such 'solutions' might range from the execution of rapists and abusers to their lengthy incarceration. In addition to dispelling such myths, this chapter illustrates how feminist thinking not only informs our abolitionist stance, but is central to it.

Chapter 5 exemplifies the many legal devices that might be used to get people off the prison track, and to avoid labeling each other 'criminal.' It also illustrates that the design and evaluation of distinct legal alternatives to treating conflicts as 'crimes' has been a particular focus among long-standing European ICOPA participants. Implicit in Slump and Emmen's report of the *dading* project is the influence of two Dutch law professors – Herman Bianchi and Louk Hulsman – who, at ICOPA I, made our capacity to put disputes into legal categories other than 'criminal' a core theme of ICOPA discussion. At ICOPA V, this tradition was placed against one more prominent in North America – an interfaith religious movement to find ways to substitute 'Restorative Justice' for criminal justice. Notable in that movement are the Canadian and US Mennonite-inspired Victim Offender Reconciliation Programs (VORPs). Different VORPs across North America and Europe channel disputes away from all stages of criminal justice processing, from pre-trial to post-imprisonment. The North American variant on decriminalization of disputes is more extra-legal than the *dading* variety, but the two approaches share the decriminalization objective.

Chapter 6 got into this manuscript by mistake and was kept by choice. Steve Russell is an enrolled Cherokee and member of the board of the Texas Indian Bar Association. In contrast to ex-prisoners Nieto and White Bird, Russell is a judge in the Texas capital, Austin. When Steve sent Hal Pepinsky a copy of his paper shortly after the conference, Hal confused him for another Texan judicial participant at ICOPA V who had opened up to the idea of abolition. By the time we discovered this mistake, we had already decided that Steve's essay nicely represents another reality recognized by ICOPA – criminal justice workers can be abolitionists too. The essay also illustrates the unity underlying various abolitionist traditions. Russell acknowledges that his sense of justice is guided by his Cherokee spiritual heritage. Yet, that sense of (in)justice finds expression in the white European thought of Michel Foucault. The power to criminalize rests in the power to surreptitiously surveille, judge, and condemn people – to know what is best for an 'offender' because, in the process, we have discovered something significant about the offender not known or understood by him/her. Such is the premise of domination – the keeper knows better than the kept what justice demands of them both. North American Native persons do not believe in having presidents and judges because they do not believe that clandestine observation and judgment facilitates any better of an understanding of someone than the understanding that person has of her/himself. In order to establish trust in the wake of conflict, conflicting parties must recognize that they share knowledge of one another; violence inherently means having to accept the world on the terms of someone whose terms are unquestionable.

In chapter 7, Finnish legal theorist, Ari Hirvonen, represents those of us who try to place ourselves in broader social and academic movements, and who try to express what underlying concern might be moving us together. He also represents a benefit which comes from having participants for whom the conference language is a second language (English through ICOPA V, Spanish and English simultaneously in ICOPA VI and VII). In using a second language, one's attention is drawn to ambiguities or connotations of words which native speakers take for granted. As the abolitionist writer self-consciously struggles to control use of the second language, so the writer becomes conscious of how language is central to what we espouse and practice. Hirvonen traces the abolitionist movement through the three phases of moralism, ideologism, and undecidability. By drawing on the work of contemporary postmodern writers, he attempts to deconstruct the narratives, or texts, of these three stages. This exercise in deconstruction will help to make the reader aware of the source of one's own ideas in the texts of 'others.' This being the case, how can a discourse of abolition be free from a discourse of repression and control? The irony identified by Hirvonen is that what appears to be an alternative discourse to repression is based in that very discourse. The discourse of the 'other' unwittingly employed by abolitionists is, ironically, the very discourse they seek to abolish. Thus the discourse of abolition, one which by definition is a discourse of negation, reinforces the discourse and practice it seeks to negate. For Hirvonen, the only way out of this impasse is for abolitionists to embark on a 'politics of undecidability.'

In chapter 8, US civil rights litigator, Frank Dunbaugh of Annapolis, Maryland, begins with a summary of successive ICOPA conferences, as he has known them since helping to organize ICOPA I. He winds up in essentially the same position as Ari and Steve, quoting the wife of a prison warden more than half a century ago:

> We obey the law, but we need respect very little of it. We must not worship any of it. It is not God. It has no sanctity .... Let the law repent its blasphemous claims ... let it throw away its

pretentious crown, and get into overalls like another servant and do its job for the community ...

Frank leads us to the practical challenge we keep facing as abolitionists: to listen most to those the system grants the least authority to be heard in the matter of what to do about a 'crime.' At the apex of the voiceless are outspoken people whose victimization is compounded by the color of their skin and by their transformation into a prisoner identity. Above all else, it is a drive to confront our ignorance about those we condemn which unites us as abolitionists, and not, as Frank, Ari, and Steve warn us against, a sense that we know what constitutes the crime problem or what is to be done about it. We presume that the body of knowledge about crime and policing is insufficient to justify further prison construction. We presume that there is not yet enough known about penal processing to halt the exploration into ways that might restore trust among disputants. This volume is but an episode in that exploration.

We want to give immediate thanks to Judy Kelley and Gina Doglione for preparing transcripts of ICOPA V sessions and converting papers into text. More generally, as you can see, we owe thanks for the conference, and for the inspiration and contents of this volume, far beyond our capacity to name you all. One exception comes immediately to mind. Little Rock Reed, who organized the Native sessions at ICOPA V, has edited some of this material in *The American Indian in the White Man's Prison: A Story of Genocide* (Vintage Books 1994). We would like to wish him well in his continuing struggles on behalf of Aboriginal peoples. We keep discovering new worlds of abolitionists ourselves. Let us not presume to give credit to all who deserve it. For our readers, any source in this volume is as good an entrée to those worlds as routes we editors and contributors followed into the field of abolition. Know that penal abolition is there for you to discover as well.

Brian MacLean
Department of Criminology
Kwantlen College
Vancouver, CANADA
V3T 5H8

Hal Pepinsky
Criminal Justice
Indiana University
Bloomington, Indiana
USA 47405

August, 1993

1 Rethinking Abolitionism: 'What Do We Do with Henry?' Review of de Haan, *The Politics of Redress*

Jim Thomas

Sharon Boehlefeld

> There is about the polemics of the prison abolitionists something of the exhilarating character which commonly infects the writing of those who are prepared to follow an argument to its logical conclusion – and beyond. (Hawkins 1976: 5)

> Nowhere is it written that kindness is preferable to cruelty. (unknown pundit)

Few people take prison abolitionists seriously, and Henry is one reason why. Henry is affable, bright, and articulate. He can also be very, very nasty, and he is currently confined in the most maximum section of Illinois' death row. Among his other crimes, he blew away one victim by inserting a shotgun into her vagina and pulling the trigger. He then slit her boyfriend's throat and left him for dead. His death sentence was commuted to life following constitutional challenges to Illinois' death penalty, but he was again sentenced to death after fatally stabbing a fellow prisoner. Confined to death row, he tried to stab yet another prisoner. Because of these and other violent acts, he is considered a danger both to staff and prisoners. Yet suggesting that there is hope even for those considered most hardened, Henry revealed some reflective self-awareness: 'I used to think I was a racist. Then I realized that I just didn't like nobody.'

All cultures face the problem of controlling intentionally violent persons who are, by overwhelming consensus, threats to social safety or

This article also appeared in *Social Justice* 18 (3), 1991: 239-251, and is reprinted here with the kind permission of the authors and *Social Justice*.

stability. Methods have varied, but few societies willingly tolerate predators. A question confronting critics of the Western model of justice is: How do we deal with Henry? Those who argue for the abolition of prisons or the reform of criminal-justice procedures are hard pressed for an answer.

In this article, we review current abolitionist thinking and assess its implications for critical criminologists in the United States. We argue that to see abolitionism as merely an idealist belief that punitive incarceration should be eliminated misses the position's value as a form of social critique. Although our own views of abolitionism remain ambivalent, we suggest that despite flaws and an often piecemeal approach to the problem of crime, the recent literature on abolition has given new impetus to critical criminology. Perhaps, as abolitionists suggest, it is time to confront the goals and future of the carceral.

The Meanings of Abolitionism

Abolitionism is a vague term that cannot be readily collapsed into a coherent, unified philosophy. At least four broadly overlapping distinctions can be made regarding the grounds on which groups oppose incarceration:

1 Ethical, rooted in Western philosophy and theological tradition;

2 Ethical, rooted in non-Western philosophy and theological tradition;

3 Anthropological, based on models of dispute resolution and decentralization; and

4 Sociological, based on the failure of the existing criminal-justice system, including incarceration, to alleviate crime problems.

These distinctions, however, apply more clearly to the arguments themselves than to those who present them. For example, in the United States, abolitionist arguments come from members of the 'peace churches,' which include Quakers (e.g., National Commission on Crime and Justice 1991), Mennonites (e.g., Zehr 1990), Justice Fellowship (Justice Fellowship 1989, 1991), and Unitarians (e.g., Unitarian Universalist Service Committee 1982). These groups employ ethics or doctrine to oppose the inhumanity of incarceration. They also draw from anthropology and sociology to develop alternatives to incarceration and to justify a need for such alternatives.

A second abolitionist variant is found in the works of thinkers who challenge the 'spirituality' of Western civilization. They suggest that the social system itself must be reorganized before we can establish a 'just society,' and that state authority and definitions of 'crime' are antithetical to social harmony, stability, and justice. Leading proponents include Quinney (1988), Quinney and Pepinsky (1990), and Pepinsky (1988), who write in the tradition of 'peace-making criminology.' Christie (1986) raises similar, fundamental questions regarding the relationship of criminal justice to human existence.

A third view exists among those who draw upon anthropological or socialist models to suggest alternate sanctioning and dispute resolution. They attack state-sponsored punishment and propose models of decentralized justice or informal mediation techniques as alternatives. This group suggests emulating systems or institutions used by other societies to replace prisons and other forms of state response to social offenses.

A fourth group – including Mathiesen (1986, 1980, 1974a, 1974b) among others (e.g., de Folter 1986; Knopp 1976; Mitford 1974; Scheerer 1986; Sommer 1976; Steinert 1986; see also back issues of *Crime and Social Justice* and the collection of essays on transcarceration in Lowman, Menzies, and Palys 1987) – employs sociological studies or social criticism to critique imprisonment and criminal-justice procedures.

Although not unified in their opposition to prisons, these groups share several broad goals. First, they recognize the disproportionate weight that minorities bear in incarceration rates. Second, they argue that minimally restrictive alternatives to imprisonment should be used to assure public safety. Finally, they argue for a restructuring of criminal law that includes decriminalization of some offenses, reclassification of behaviors not amenable to deterrence (such as drug abuse), and substitution of non-criminal responses for acts that are not a direct threat to public safety. These disparate bits of the abolitionist mosaic do not form a consistent pattern of theoretical or conceptual logic, but they nonetheless create an image of one potential solution to the prison problem.

The Progenitor of Contemporary Abolitionism: Thomas Mathiesen

The intellectual exemplar for most abolitionist thinking is Thomas Mathiesen, who for nearly a quarter century has articulated thoughtful and powerful arguments against prisons. In *The Politics of Abolition*, perhaps his most influential work, Mathiesen analyzes the activities of various Scandinavian abolitionist/reform groups. Although he is self-consciously vague about his ultimate abolitionist goals and gives compelling reasons for this vagueness, he is explicitly clear in his support for 'non-reformist reforms.' The term, borrowed from Gorz (1968), refers to implementing changes that are not merely cosmetic, but possess the potential for structural transformation:

> A reformist reform is one that subordinates its objectives to the criteria of rationality and practicability of a given system and policy. Reformism rejects those objectives and demands – however deep the need for them – which are incompatible with the preservation of the system.
>
> On the other hand, a not necessarily reformist reform is one that is conceived not in terms of what is possible within the framework of a given system and administration, but in view of what should be made possible in terms of human needs and demands …. A non-reformist reform is determined not in terms of what can be, but what should be. (ibid.: 7-8)

Accordingly, Mathiesen emphasizes a dialectical relationship between political action and social change. His spatial metaphors (e.g., 'insiders/outsiders,' 'upwards/sideways') suggest ways to transform parts of a (prison) system while working toward eventual abolition.

Mathiesen (1986: 88-93) lists eight arguments that collectively 'constitute a forceful basis for advocating a policy of a permanent international ban on prison building:'

1 Imprisonment does not prevent those incarcerated from committing subsequent crimes. We do not need 'more of the same.'

2 Prison effectiveness in deterring crime is uncertain and less significant than other social factors that might achieve the same result.

3 Prison overcrowding should be addressed by confining fewer prisoners, and not by building more prisons.

4 Prisons possess an irreversible character, such that if they exist, they will be used. The danger lies in maintaining a population to utilize their existence.

5 Prison expansion is driven by a political ethos that fosters expansion, taking on a momentum that is difficult to stop.

6 Prisons are inhumane.

7 Cultural values embedded in the conception of prisons reflect a social ethos of violence and degradation. When prisons are expanded, so too are negative cultural values symbolizing acceptable strategies for resolving interpersonal conflict.

8 Prisons are not cost effective.

As Scheerer (1986: 9) reminds us, a body of abolitionist literature does not automatically make a theory. Despite the occasional compelling and articulate abolitionist works of the past two decades, only recently has there been a serious attempt to move beyond Mathiesen and integrate diverse perspectives into a comprehensive theory of practice. Willem de Haan, in recognizing abolitionism as a 'sensitizing' concept and in combining competing ideas, attempts to develop a synthetic position by which critical thinkers can more firmly ground opposition to prisons.

De Haan on Abolition

The core of de Haan's argument in *The Politics of Redress* is that abolitionism can enlarge the theoretical scope for assessing and developing social responses to social offenses. His work is simultaneously ambitious, flawed, provocative, and important. He grapples with abolitionist questions and suggests an inchoate critical framework by which to reassess the tenets of abolitionism, build upon its strengths, and modify its weaknesses. The failure of critical criminologists to take abolition seriously provides the entry for de Haan's formulation of the concept of 'redress,' which he sees as a more just response to crime and punishment.

De Haan begins with the (correct) premise that few critical criminologists have logically concluded that prisons should be abolished. Although somewhat oversimplified, his argument is as follows: the criminal-justice systems of Western democracies are unjust; critical scholars, while developing a variety of sophisticated theories, have failed to address successfully how society should respond to social offenses; punishment is wrong and 'redress' is better; further, we can begin developing an ethically informed theoretical justification for abolition by borrowing from Habermas' concept of 'communicative ethics.'

Rather than view behaviors as 'criminal,' de Haan (1990: 158) argues that we should instead reconceptualize them as 'undesirable events,' which would direct criminological discourse away from legally defined offenses and prescribed punitive measures and toward problem solving.

It is not clear how some forms of redress would avoid being simply punishment by another name whenever both cause suffering, but for the purposes of his argument this is of minor significance.

Although the bulk of de Haan's data comes from the Netherlands, he draws liberally from other countries to raise his discussion to the level of an international critique. He pulls together literature unavailable to most US scholars, whose insularity and ethnocentrism constrain them to their own experience and English-speaking sources.

The most provocative, although underdeveloped, set of ideas introduced by de Haan proposes 'communication ethics' as the basis of a theory and practice of abolitionist values. Drawing especially from Habermas' theory of communicative action (e.g., Habermas 1979, 1984), de Haan suggests that we can construct a rationalist ethical theory based on universal consensus.[1]

A Habermasian Framework for Abolitionism?

For Habermas (1975: 87), individual morality is sanctioned only through the inner authority of conscience, and even when in conflict with the polity, such principles are embedded in a claim to universality. Habermas rejects a Kantian formalistic ethics in favor of 'communicative ethics,' 'which guarantees the generality of admissible norms and the autonomy of acting subjects solely through the discursive redeemability of the validity claims with which norms appear' (ibid.: 89). For Habermas, only communicative ethics are universal and guarantee consensual 'will formation' by the polity in shaping and validating social values through rational critique.

Habermas' rationalist liberalism, which guides his theory of communication, is founded on the premise that consensus is possible within a social system and culture based on free and unconstrained dialogue between communicants. In such an 'ideal speech community,' reason prevails, norms reflect the needs of the society rather than the imposition of ideological and repressive conceptual machinery, and the principles of the Enlightenment can be advanced. Communicative rationality integrates segmented spheres of the life world such that claims to 'truth' and 'ethics' become discursively solvable.

Moving from communicative action to abolition and redress, however, requires a leap of faith to claim that something embedded in Enlightenment principles would logically lead to the conclusion that prisons must be abolished. In this sense, an *a priori* assumption of consequence seems philosophically idealistic, even Platonic, in that an outcome is preordained because of the belief that rational people would necessarily accept the idealized value of 'reducing suffering' when sanctioning undesirable behavior.

Such a synthesis is impressive, though difficult, and to achieve it de Haan minimizes the problems in Habermas' communication theory, including concepts such as 'universal pragmatics,' 'consensual validation,' or 'communication competence.' He is also vague on how one moves from a culture based on values that emphasize punitive discourse and an ethics of retribution to one based on a partially articulated ethics of 'justice' and redress. However, often the value of a work lies not in the clarity with which an issue is advanced, but in the very fact that the idea is advanced at all. De Haan's analysis provides considerable material for thought and debate as scholars confront its problems and potential.

The Critique of de Haan

A strength of de Haan's work is that it raises more questions than it answers. One leaves his work asking: Is there, or should there be, a distinction between scientific and philosophical argument? If there is a distinction, is it possible to refute a philosophical stance in the same way as a scientific theory can be refuted? Do the answers to these questions have a direct bearing on policy decisions of criminal-justice practitioners, who tend to be influenced by social and fiscal pressures? Is liberal moral philosophy (of which, we believe, Rawls and Habermas are proponents) really so impoverished as to offer no building blocks on which to ground abolitionism? De Haan would answer yes to each of these questions, but the problem of implementation remains.

Unfortunately, de Haan never provides a clear definition of abolitionism. Do we tear down all prisons, or do we simply use confinement in extreme cases? He seems to argue for the former while leaving open the possibility of the latter. On the one hand, he argues that we need to make the case 'more stringently why punishment can never be justified, not only under the present circumstances, but, indeed, never ever' (de Haan 1990: 127). On the other hand, he argues that the basis for this claim can be derived from 'discourse ethics,' a position that hardly allows such a conclusion to be imposed prior to consensual validation of universal norms.

Neither does he give a coherent rationale for preferring abolition to continued incarceration that others such as Mathiesen have attempted. We are not told how sanctions differ from punishment, or what redress means as a practical strategy in dealing with criminal, rather than civil, offenses. De Haan critiques the transferability thesis, which holds that models of dispute resolution from other cultures can be modified and introduced into Western culture. His ambivalence about the thesis is reflected in his apparent suspicion of socialist legality, which some scholars of Cuba and China have suggested as an alternative for Western societies. Using Cuba as an example, however, he develops a perspective – rather than an alternative – for engaging in ideological struggles over criminal justice (ibid.: 149).

There are other nagging problems that remain unaddressed. What happens when we decarcerate? There is, for example, evidence that deinstitutionalizing the mentally ill, a position supported by the Left and cynically exploited during the Reagan era, created more, rather than less, suffering. Further, as Teplin (1990) argued in her study of Cook County (Ill.) jail, the prevalence of severely mentally disordered inmates increased following deinstitutionalization. Although the analogy is not perfect, it challenges the claim that deinstitutionalizing the criminal-justice system without creating alternate structures would, in fact, lead to less suffering. Would decarceration lead to an increase in capital punishment for the most violent offenders such that abolishing prisons would be a pyrrhic victory?

Reading the *Politics of Redress* evokes images of the light brigade charging into the valley of death in a noble, but futile battle. De Haan faces a prodigious and unenviable task, and the ambitiousness of the task and his willingness to attempt it alone are enough to inspire our admiration. He confronts the readers with several ways to reframe abolitionist thinking and his work is invaluable as a way of launching a new critique on the repressive ethos of punishment as we enter the 21st century.

Why Bother with Abolitionism?

We need fewer prisons. Of the primary functions of prison – incapacitation, punishment, deterrence, stigmatization, and rehabilitation – only incapacitation cannot be served by alternate methods. Walker's (1980) critique of the justifications for imposing penalties identifies problems with these functions, suggesting that even if all were effective, they might be incompatible.

Prisons fail to rehabilitate not because of the general intransigence of inmates, but because the structure and lack of programs, particularly in maximum-security institutions, subvert the rehabilitative ideal. The literature on deterrence remains mixed on the statistical relationship between sanctions and offense. Punishment may make us feel better, but it has no tangible effect on criminal behavior, and the debilitating conditions of prison may actually increase crime by releasing persons even less equipped to deal with their society than they were when they entered.

Even the incapacitation justification seems only marginally convincing. Although annual statistics may vary slightly, a general trend over the past decade is clear. Less than 40% of victimization offenses are reported to police (*Bureau of Justice Statistics Bulletin* 1988: 2), and only about 20% of known crimes are cleared by arrest (*CJS Sourcebook* 1989: 449). The *CJS Sourcebook* shows that of those arrested, about 80% are prosecuted, three-quarters of those prosecuted are convicted, and about 70% of all felony convictions result in a prison or jail sentence. Consequently, only three persons are incarcerated (in prisons or jails) for every 100 crimes committed.[2]

Austin (1986) and Irwin and Austin (1987) argue that shorter, rather than longer, sentences may not only *not* lead to more crime, but also may save money. For example, in Illinois, during a temporary early release program from 1980 to 1983, the crime rate declined while the policy was in effect and the state saved almost $50 million. In short, most offenders are not 'incapacitated' and remain on the streets. Incapacitating a few at high cost seems to have little (if any) positive effect on the crime rate. Abolitionists must adduce further evidence to strengthen these claims, in order to challenge the ideological justification for prisons as a response to serious social offenses.

Taking Abolition Seriously

Abolitionists carry a stigma. They are perceived to be unrealistic, naïve, and impractical dreamers who believe that if we think nice thoughts, then social menaces will disappear. This perception, although perhaps sometimes justified, is generally unfair.

Utilitarian philosophy may inform justice procedures, but the ideological foundation of contract, rights, fairness, and autonomy derives from 17th- and 18th-century philosophers from Locke to Kant in particular. Rawls' (1971) attempt to develop a neo-Kantian theory of justice as fairness is consistent with both Habermas' conception of communicative ethics and abolitionists' commitment to Enlightenment principles. The most significant difference is that abolitionists, as Hawkins (1976: 5) observes, arrive at their conclusion without worrying about either establishing their premises or the mundane practical problems the conclusion entails. It is time for a 'realist neo-abolitionism' that builds on the core ideas of such thinkers as Mathiesen and de Haan. Such a neo-abolitionism would move beyond rhetoric to developing theoretical and empirical insights. It would substitute strident calls to 'tear down the walls' with realistic proposals recognizing the need to protect society from the worst predators while offering alternatives for other offenders.

Abolitionist thinking offers critical criminologists several sensitizing themes. First, it directly confronts the cynicism and anomie of postmodernists with an insistence on expanding the limits of Enlightenment ideals. The notion of progress, a commitment to universalistic values, and the belief that social action may improve social existence provide an antidote to the postmodernists' neo-nihilism. If abolitionists were to confront their own premises more self-consciously, they could articulate a formidable theoretical system.

Second, a strong cadre of abolitionists would make even more visible the simple truth that prisons don't work – either as punishment or as means of ensuring the safety and stability of the commonweal. Too many leftists complain about disproportional incarceration rates that send the poor and the deprived to prison. This is noble. The complaint, however, implies that if incarceration rates were fair, then the carceral would be acceptable. Abolitionists do not complain that the poor are in prison, while also arguing that we should imprison the Savings and Loan offenders, the Contragate participants, or our most disliked category of offenders (e.g., rapists, drunk drivers). The abolitionist goal is not to make prisons more just, but to eliminate them entirely. This would require the Left to seriously consider precisely what it would do with social offenders, and although it risks further expanding the schisms between various leftist groups, it would bring the *sub-rosa* philosophical disputes into the open where they could be assessed and debated.[3]

Third, abolitionist thinking, especially as formulated by de Haan in his contention that a communicative ethics provides a theoretical grounding, can potentially reshape the terrain of discourse of critical criminology. It is nice to be nice, but why? An ethically informed theoretical foundation that guides research and policy would sharpen critical think-

ing and move it beyond the current dilemma of chosing between reformist liberalism and strident polemics, both of which have place, but
neither of which seems eminently satisfying.

Finally, a coherent abolitionist position, as de Haan implies, may
integrate a variety of diverse intellectual traditions including neo-Kan-
tians (e.g., Rawls), critical theorists (e.g., Habermas), Marxists, and many
others. The goal for neo-abolitionists is to reclaim the ethical high ground
and engage more aggressively in debating the existence of prisons:

> Improvements seem to be achievable only if enough people can
> be persuaded to adopt moral positions which are both simple
> and extreme: the assertion of inalienable rights, the disowning of
> deterrence, the abandonment of treatment, the denial of danger-
> ousness. What is disquieting is not merely the reduction of
> penology to a political level, in which rhetoric takes the place of
> reasoning. It is the very real possibility that the whole subject
> will be discredited both amongst practitioners – by which I mean
> sentencers, administrators, and those whose job it is to handle
> offenders – and also in the eyes of research workers and moral
> philosophers who, if not disillusioned, would make genuine
> contributions. (Walker 1980: 189)

Conclusion

The basis of abolitionism lies in Enlightenment principles and an explicit
humanism that, while noble, cannot be uncritically accepted in light of
postmodernist critiques that challenge the notion of progress, emancipation, and universalistic norms and values. The Kantian basis of the
implied categorical imperative in which abolitionism would be recognized by all 'right-thinking' folk, once they looked at the problem
reasonably, rests on the assumption that the goals of official policies
necessarily reflect the commonweal. How does one deal with the
argument that rejects all rational arguments and falls back on punitive
revenge as its own justification?

Those who look to other cultures or other times for models of dispute
resolution have much to contribute. However, there is too little caution,
especially among leftists who idealize socialist models of justice, about
romanticizing decentralization. As Mika (1987) has argued, the 'myth of
community' creates fuzzy views of solidarity, and 'neighborhoods'
might be as much an ideological fiction as a consensual conceptual
reality. In addition, in socialist and other models of justice, many

offenses relegated to informal or decentralized systems are minor. The prison systems of socialist countries are hardly an ideal model to implement, and societies with some forms of mediation also rely on harsher corporal or capital punishment (often draconian by Enlightenment standards) for serious offenses.

We come full circle: If we abolish prisons, what do we do with Henry? Our answer is that for now, it doesn't matter. We side with Mathiesen and others who argue that for the nonce we face three tasks. First, we must reform prisons, the justice system, social-control procedures, and society along the lines of Enlightenment principles that emphasize ethical, spiritual, and material rejuvenation so as to eliminate unnecessary forms of social domination. Second, we must reclaim the ethical and practical high ground and move beyond liberal reform by clearly articulating a theoretical and practical justification – building on the works of Mathiesen, de Haan, and others – for abolishing prisons as a *primary* mechanism of punishment. Finally, we must remind ourselves that struggle is as long as history, and that the outcomes of our resistance to unjust forms of social control are rarely immediately visible. Instead of moving toward the center, it is time abolitionists aggressively move toward the cutting edge by going beyond rhetoric and staking out firmer theoretical ground.

NOTES

1 The discussion here derives from Habermas, not de Haan, because de Haan limits his discussion to the kernel, rather than to a complete outline, of Habermas' position.

2 These figures are illustrative and far from precise. Some offenders commit multiple offenses, which skews the incarceration rate slightly upwards. However, many crimes included in the prosecution, conviction, and incarceration figures, such as drug offenses, are 'victimless' and generally are not reported or known to police. This makes it appear as though we are locking 'criminals' up by conflating crimes that are reported by victims (either officially or in victimization surveys) with victimless crimes that are not. Substance-abuse offenses are the overwhelming cause for the increase of both federal and state prison and jail populations. One can quibble over classification and calculation, but the point remains that few serious offenders are in prison.

3 The debates with feminists who argue for harsh sentences for crimes of violence against women are especially contentious. However, we must not retreat from applying the same standards to these as to all other offenses by asking not how we punish, but rather how we are to respond.

REFERENCES

Austin, James. 1986. 'Using Early Release to Relieve Prison Crowding: A Dilemma in Public Policy.' *Crime and Delinquency*, 32 (October): 404-501

Bureau of Justice Statistics Bulletin. 1990. 'Felony Sentences in State Courts.' Washington, DC: US Department of Justice

Christie, Nils. 1986. 'Images of Man in Modern Penal Law.' *Contemporary Crises*, 10 (1): 95-115

de Folter, Rolf S. 1986. 'On the Methodological Foundation of the Abolitionist Approach to the Criminal Justice System: A Comparison of the Ideas of Hulsman, Mathiesen, and Foucault.' *Contemporary Crisis*, 10 (1): 39-62

de Haan, Willem. 1990. *The Politics of Redress: Crime, Punishment, and Penal Abolition.* Boston: Unwin Hyman

Gorz, Andre. 1968. *Strategy for Labor: A Radical Proposal.* Boston: Beacon Press

Habermas, Jurgen. 1984. *The Theory of Communicative Action*, Volume 1: *Reason and the Rationalization of Society.* Boston: Beacon Press

– 1979. *Communication and the Evolution of Society.* Boston: Beacon Press

– 1975. *Legitimation Crisis.* Boston: Beacon Press

Hawkins, Gordon. 1976. *The Prison: Policy and Practice.* Chicago: Chicago University Press

Irwin, John and James Austin. 1987. *It's about Time: Solving America's Prison Overcrowding Crisis.* San Francisco: National Council on Crime and Delinquency

Justice Fellowship. 1991. *Beyond Crime and Punishment.* Washington: Prison Fellowship

– 1989. *Is There a Better Way?* Washington: Prison Fellowship

Knopp, Fay Honey. 1976. *Instead of Prisons: A Handbook for Abolitionists.* Syracuse, New York: Prison Research Education Action Project

Lowman, John, Robert J. Menzies, and T.S. Palys, eds. 1987. *Transcarceration: Essays in the Sociology of Social Control*. Aldershot, England: Gower

Mathiesen, Thomas. 1986. 'The Politics of Abolition.' *Contemporary Crisis*, 10 (1): 81-94

– 1980. *Law, Society and Political Action: Towards a Strategy under Late Capitalism*. New York: Academic Press

– 1974a. *The Politics of Abolition: Essays in Political Action Theory*. London: Martin Robertson

– 1974b. 'The Prison Movement in Scandinavia.' *Crime and Social Justice*, 1 (Spring-Summer): 45-50

Mauer, Marc. 1991. *Americans Behind Bars: A Comparison of International Rates of Incarceration*. Washington: The Sentencing Project (American Friends Service Committee)

– 1988. 'Doing Good Instead of Doing Time.' *Business and Society Review*, 66 (Summer): 22-25

Mika, Harry. 1987. 'Mediating Neighborhood Conflict: Conceptual and Strategic Considerations.' *Negotiation Journal*, 3 (October): 397-410

Mitford, Jessica. 1974. *Kind and Unusual Punishment: The Prison Business*. New York: Vintage Press

National Commission on Crime and Justice. 1991. *A Call to Action: An Analysis and Overview of the United States Criminal Justice System, with Recommendations*. Philadelphia: National Commission on Crime and Justice (AFSC)

Pepinsky, Harold. 1988. 'Violence as Unresponsiveness: Toward a New Conception of Crime.' *Justice Quarterly*, 5 (December): 539

Platt, Tony, and Paul Takagi, eds. 1982. *Law and Order in the 1980s: The Rise of the Right*. San Francisco: Synthesis Press

Quinney, Richard. 1988. 'Crime, Suffering, Service: Toward a Criminology of Peacemaking.' *The Quest*: 66-75

Quinney, Richard, and Harold E. Pepinsky, eds. 1990. *The Theory and Practice of Peacemaking in the Development of Radical Criminology*. Bloomington: IN University Press

Rawls, John. 1971. *A Theory of Justice*. Cambridge, MASS: Harvard University Press

Scheerer, Sebastian. 1986. 'Towards Abolitionism.' *Contemporary Crises*, 10 (1): 5-20

Sommer, Robert. 1976. *The End of Imprisonment.* New York: Oxford University Press

Sourcebook of Criminal Justice Statistics. 1990. *1989 Installment.* Washington, DC: US Department of Justice

Steinert, Heinz. 1986. 'Beyond Crime and Punishment.' *Contemporary Crises,* 10 (1): 21-38

Teplin, Linda A. 1990. 'The Prevalence of Severe Mental Disorder among Male Urban Jail Detainees: Comparison with the Epidemiologic Catchment Area Program.' *American Journal of Public Health,* 80 (6): 663-669

Tomasic, Roman and Malcolm M. Feeley. 1982. *Neighborhood Justice: Assessment of an Emerging Idea.* New York: Longman

Walker, Nigel. 1980. *Punishment, Danger and Stigma: The Morality of Criminal Justice.* Totowa, NJ: Barnes and Noble

Unitarian Universalist Service Committee. 1982. *Alternatives to Imprisonment: A Thoughtful Approach to Crime and Punishment.* Boston: Unitarian Universalist Service Committee

Zehr, Howard. 1990. *Mediating the Victim-Offender Conflict: The Victim Offender Rehabilitation Program.* Akron, PA.: US Mennonite Control Committee

2   On the Death Penalty and Abolition

Bob Gross

The headquarters of the National Coalition to Abolish the Death Penalty
(NCAP) is in Washington, DC, although, during an interim period, it was
in Liberty, Indiana. A number of you here in the room are involved with
the National Coalition, and our executive committee, and others of you
have been to our conferences and our workshops. The NCAP is a
coalition of organizations at a national level – about sixty national
organizations from all the major churches, civil rights and human rights
groups, legal advocacy groups, and other public interest groups. We also
have coalitions at the state and local level, such as the Indiana Coalition
Against the Death Penalty and the Eastern Missouri Coalition Against
the Death Penalty. Local and state coalitions are equal partners in the
national coalition.

NCAP works at both the national and the grassroots levels. I want to
give a quick overview of what I think has been a general flow of how
people have been working and what strategies folks have used for
abolition over the last several years. Initially the response was primarily
legal when the Supreme Court re-established the death penalty in 1977.
For example a hundred people were taken off death row in the early
1980s by one court case. Individual states had similar experiences so that
some cases represent major steps forward in a particular state or even
nationally in terms of one legal issue.

As time has gone on, we have had some folks like Nixon, Reagan, and
Bush appointing judges at the federal level, and the courts are not as easy

to work with on anything related to our concerns – the death penalty or many others. Thus, the courts are probably not our current primary source of relief on this problem. Besides, many of those *big* issues have been litigated and have been resolved and the death penalty has cleaned up its act, so to speak, in terms of the most blatant abuses. I sometimes say that maybe the most extreme 10 percent of the arbitrary use of the death penalty may be gone now; but, the bulk of it remains. For example, examine the difference between the *Furman* decision in 1972, and the *McCluskey* decision in 1989. In 1972 the court ruled that there seems to be a real possibility that the use of the death penalty is discriminatory by race. They ruled that since there is a real possibility of arbitrary discrimination, we must cease with executions. Seventeen years later, the Court says, 'Well you have proven this an observable, documented pattern of discrimination in the way the death penalty is used but it does not matter in Warren McCluskey's case. He has to prove that his judge, prosecutor, and jury intended to discriminate against him because he is an African American, and perhaps because his victim was white. And so the fact that you have proven the death penalty is discriminatory does not matter.' If the 1972 court had heard the case presented in *McCluskey*, we might not have a death penalty today. So much for the legal strategy.

The public education strategy has always been followed. We see public education as the primary means to make legislators change their minds, even in order for courts, I think, to change their rulings. It might be flippant, but probably true, to say that the courts read the newspapers as closely as they do the Constitution, and neither one as closely as they do other kinds of evidence. Public education is the key to everything we can accomplish. Legislative strategy is linked to public education. We work incrementally at times, as with the bill that would exempt the mentally retarded from the death penalty in Georgia, or we introduce a bill that would raise the minimum age of people who could be subject to the death penalty in Indiana.

One direction gaining much strength is direct action in simple, straightforward witness, although people have been doing it all along. Howard Zehr of the Mennonite Central Committee (formally in Elkhart, Indiana, now in Akron, Pennsylvania) could tell you about things that a group called 'HEX' was doing ten years ago that are still going on – sometimes extra-legal ways of witnessing against the death penalty. A few years ago, a movement to hold marches in a more widely defined direct action with much broader participation has developed. Direct action brings a spirit into the movement that has enlivened every other abolition strategy.

Through the decades, public opinion polls have asked, 'In general, do you favor or oppose capital punishment?' The proportion of those in favor have climbed from just under 50 percent in the early 1960s, to approximately 75 percent now. But surveys are not the only way to measure public attitudes towards the death penalty, and survey data can be superficial.

In the last three or four years polling techniques have become more sophisticated. Some give facts of a case and ask the respondent, if they were on the jury, would they vote for death or another particular sentence. Some polls ask the respondent if people under the age of 21, or under the age of 18, at the time of the crime should be sentenced to death. Other polls have asked respondents if people who are fundamentally handicapped, mentally retarded, or mentally ill should be executed. Still other polls ask respondents if someone who did not pull the trigger but is somehow involved in the crime should be executed. Every time you introduce these categories, which make up a surprisingly large segment of who is on death row, you find people responding, 'Well I guess not them, I guess not for those people.' These results make us feel more hopeful about popular opinion pertaining to the death penalty. Additionally, the results of the polls are politically useful. For instance, 52 percent of the people in Georgia would abolish the death penalty, if the alternative were a 25-year minimum sentence with some kind of restitution to victims' families. That gives you something to say to the Georgia legislature or to the Georgia public: Georgians want the alternatives rather than the death penalty. That means a whole lot more than talking about how wrong it is, how discriminatory it is, how costly it is, or something else. Some people will side with you just to be atypical. I am not a very good sheep in the flock, but it seems that most people are. For me, it is comforting to know my inner doubts about the death penalty are shared by a majority of my neighbors. The death penalty is the result of politics, not because it keeps us safer. On the whole, decision makers probably do not believe that idea themselves. Capital punishment is not necessarily an important issue to the public because if you ask voters what issues matter to them, the death penalty does not even make the list. Political candidates make the death penalty an issue because they want to ride into office on the whole complex cluster of fears and reactive patterns that people have. Let me provide you with an example.

A few years ago in California, the Supreme Court required that strict, legal principle be observed and were not affirming any death sentences. At the same time, the Court did not give the green light to big business developing in parts of California. The Court were very conservationist and environmentalist in their legal interpretation. The Court has to be reconfirmed periodically by election and the members of this Court were ultimately kicked out of office. They were kicked out because big business could not live with their environmental conservationism. Capital punishment became the pretext. If you portray anyone – a judge or a politician or whoever – as protecting the redwoods, you have not slandered her/him. If you portray the individual as protecting criminals, then you have something. You have something that can be used to frighten people, and you can get them to respond: 'Well, let's get rid of this Court and maybe we won't have so much murder.' Millions of dollars were spent in discrediting that court. Capital punishment worked politically. Now Californians have much more fear of crime and much more of a sense that the death penalty is somehow an answer.

Willie Horton is a parallel example. We did not elect a president on the basis of his policies about prison furloughs. We elected a president because that was an issue that could frighten white people. What we have to do then, is to negate that issue. We need voter awareness of the nature of the game. Politicians are trying to buy your vote at the expense of your own safety. They are not concerned about you, they are concerned about your vote. One thing in our favor is that politicians are not highly credible to the public. For different reasons, neither are abolitionists, but if we align with the people, build alliances and connections and tell them that 'You've got to watch these people, they will sell you something in which they don't even believe just to get your vote, even if they know it doesn't work,' then we might get to a point where we have some real leaders with some real solutions to the problems of violent crime.

The good news is that their strategy did not work in the 1990 election. Virtually every politician in all parts of the country who tried to use the death penalty in such a crude way, to ride that fear and harsh response into office, was defeated. This gives us real hope.

Delbert Tibbs

I happen to have been on death row. I am one of the fortunate few to escape it. When my case was overturned by the Florida Supreme Court, it was a four-to-three decision that I should not have been convicted based on the evidence that was presented at my trial – that someone said I did it, and I said I did not. I wonder why the three justices thought I did it while the other four did not. These people all went to prestigious law schools and come from the same culture. Why would they arrive at such diametrically opposed conclusions? And the one thing that presents itself is consciousness. I would bet that at least three of the four who over-turned my conviction were Democrats. The four who let me go were moderately liberal and so forth, while the justices who voted to uphold my death sentence saw a black man accused of raping a white woman. Porter Kirkwood told a story earlier in this conference which I am going to repeat. A young man in North Carolina was out drinking with his friends one night. He came home late, did not want to disturb his parents, and did not want them to see him drunk. So he crawled through a window of a house that looked like his house and he fell asleep. Except it was not his house. It was a white family's house in the next block. They came in the next morning and saw this Negro in their baby daughter's room laid out on the floor. I can picture it in my mind: folks are screaming and stuff and they call the police. The guy explained, but they charged him with rape even though the doctor examined the young woman and found no indication of any kind of sexual trauma or activity at all.

Porter went on to say that the reason this system exists is to teach you a lesson: do not get caught in a circumstance, even by accident. He could have raped someone even if did not. And they may have even thought he probably wanted to rape someone. We all know that from the 1930s to the 1960s there were approximately 400 executions for rape in this country, most of them in the South. In about 90 per cent of these cases, black men were accused of raping white women. That is what the three dissenting justices saw when they saw me and thought 'uppity nigger from up north, who didn't act like he was from the South and didn't act like he was supposed to act if he is a black person born in the South.' You know how to act. You know not look too directly at folks, not to be too assertive. I did not have enough sense to know not to do any of these things. A friend of mine, who is a white woman, was doing some investigative work on my case and found several contradictions which she presented to the judge. I hugged and kissed her in the courtroom during recess. Then I realized what I had done and said, 'Oh my God!' This is the kind of consciousness that supports the death penalty.

Claire Regan

I want to talk about education. I came to Amnesty International because I do a lot of educating on this issue and Amnesty needed a Western New York Anti-Death Penalty Coordinator.

My main effort is with the Judicial Process Commission which is part of the Ecumenical Ministries in Rochester. We work with editorial boards of newspapers to give them good facts and figures. They are often coming from the same emotional positions as the general public. If you can convince *them*, you can convince others. We have had better luck with the editorial boards than we ever had with some of the legislators, although I will say that Rochester is the place that put the death penalty on hold for at least two years in New York. Last year the New York legislature came within one vote of over ridding the governor's veto of a bill that re-introduced the death penalty. As soon as Cuomo leaves and we have a governor who wants the death penalty, New York will join the other death penalty states. And we have had two things happen. A state senator, James Donavan, who has always been in favor of the death penalty, has cancer, and was on his death bed or knew he was going to die soon and decided he was not going to meet his maker without an act of mercy. So when it came time to vote to over ride Cuomo's veto, he was nowhere to be seen. They needed his vote to over ride so they did not try it first in the Senate. And in the assembly, it was very, very close.

One legislator from Rochester, who had always voted against the death penalty, had decided he was in favour because he got them to add some amendments to say that no innocent people would ever be executed. When he ran for re-election, we had a young woman running against him. He was also anti-abortion and she was pro-choice. It was sort of funny: she was pro-choice, anti-death penalty and he had switched the other way. He was defeated. Another woman, with whom we talked, would say 'I'm personally against the death penalty but I have to do what my constituents want,' was defeated by someone who was against the death penalty. So we had a two-vote cushion in the Rochester area and there was one more person from New York City who had been pro-death penalty who was replaced by someone who was anti-death penalty. So we feel that we are safe for two years. And that is about as much as we can say.

How do you educate and what is the best way? I go out and speak to churches when I can get invited. I go out and speak to schools when I get a chance. Each August I send a letter around with my credentials. I do not tell them that I have never had a criminal justice course or a sociology course and that I am educated as a chemist. I tell them what groups I belong to and how long I have been in the field, that sort of thing. I will speak to classes two days in a row, six classes in a row if necessary. I have done English classes where there are going to be debates. I have done government classes, I have done health classes. For years I went into health classes to talk about alternatives to prisons and the death penalty to say that the death penalty has always been unhealthy, and that prison is not very healthy either. You have to be pretty flexible. If they want me in a calculus class, I will go. I tell them I will talk to them on alternatives to prison, drug legalization or the death penalty. Recently the death penalty has been the favorite subject.

There is so much misinformation on who executes, and more and more countries are abolishing the death penalty. For the countries that still retain it, I offer the latest date and point to reliable sources. The NAACP Legal Defense Fund puts out a list of people on death row about four times a year. As of 24 April, 1991, there were 2457 people on death row in the United States. They tell you the race of the defendant, which jurisdictions have the death penalty, and which do not. They look at the race of the people executed and the race of their victims. We have executed 145 people since Gary Gilmore in 1977. Only 20 of these cases had exclusively minority victims, although minorities make up half of all murder victims. If you kill a white person, as I recall you are six times more likely to be given a death penalty in Colorado than if you kill a black. If you are a black person who kills a white person, you are much more likely to be executed than if you are a white person who kills a white person or if you are a black person who kills a black person.

People are very surprised when I name the countries that execute or intend to execute. China is number one. Over a six-month period in 1988/89, there were 900 executions in Iran, and 700 in Iraq. A lot of political prisoners and drug offenders were executed.

They stone people to death for sex crimes there. I go into some of the descriptions of stoning which are not real pretty. They dress offenders in white, including a white hood. They take a truckload of stones to a stadium for audience participation. The law is that no one stone can be big enough to kill. You get to go out and pick up your stone and get your hit. Of course the person in white eventually becomes bloody. The person falls down. They continue to stone. When they think the person is dead someone takes a shovel or stick, hits the person on the head, and then takes him or her away.

We know that we do not do things like that in the United States. Then you can use the NAACP's current list of 14 or 15 botched executions. Where the electric chair is not hooked up properly, or it is not functioning correctly, and we have to give several jolts of electricity, you can describe a little bit about what happens. With one woman executed prior to Gary Gilmore, the executioner went in to take the body out, did not put on gloves, and got second-degree burns. The brain boils and the eyes melt. In Michigan in 1860 they hanged a guy. They had not adjusted the rope properly and four people had to drag down on him for about 11 minutes before he strangled to death. The governor's wife witnessed this botched execution, was strongly affected by it, and so they abolished the death penalty, even until today.

If you get the knot too tight it decapitates the person, which does not bother the person being killed, but it does bother some of the observers. We think that the guillotine is a little too primitive, and so we use lethal injection. They strap you to a gurney and it could be quick. If you have an operation, and they give you sodium pentothal, you count back from 100 (I get to about 96) and you are unconscious. Then if you give sodium chloride and a muscle relaxant to stop the heart. But James Autry (the first to be executed in Texas after 1977) was conscious on the gurney for 10 minutes as they were pouring the stuff into him. Many people who have been strapped on the gurney are drug users? Their veins are collapsed. Executioners use big catheters and they jab some of these people for 30 or 40 minutes trying to find a vein. Any of you who are not terribly into injections, think of someone poking you with a big needle for that length of time. That may be cruel and unusual too. One time, the catheter flew out and started spraying people around the room, so they pulled the curtains and people could hear the guy moaning. It was about twenty minutes before they got him hooked up properly again.

They still use gas in some places. Gas is also fairly painful and the condemned choke to death. Jimmy Gray was beating his head on the post for about eight minutes before he finally became unconscious, and some of the people viewing it fainted. If people think execution is something neat and clean, they may be disabused of that idea.

Some people argue that the death penalty is a deterrent. There are numerous studies indicating that rather than capital punishment being a deterrent, the murder rate goes up after an execution. William Bowers and Dunne Pierce from Northeastern University, for example, have found that, in New York from 1906 to 1963, there were 600 people executed. Two additional murders are documented in the state in the months following each execution. People were quite surprised by this finding and argued that the data must be faulty. So the researchers looked at California, the Dakotas, and Virginia and they found the same trend.

Most murders are not going to be deterred because they are not premeditated. They are usually between family members and friends. Your kid asks you for the car keys and you say, 'No way.' There are lovers quarrels, husband and wives, people sitting out on the stoops on a hot night drinking beer and someone insults someone else's lady friend. I also believe, although I cannot prove it, that when the state uses violence to solve its problems, it seems to give some unstable people permission to kill, as does war. There are also a large number of people out there who are suicidal and who do not have the determination to kill themselves. Gary Gilmore had tried to commit suicide several times. I cannot defend any murder: Gilmore went into two places, tied the clerk up, robbed people and then put bullets through their heads. He did not fight his execution. He not only tried to commit suicide again, but, he also tried to convince his girlfriend to commit suicide because, if he could not have her, then he did not want anyone else to have her either. She very nearly died before they got to her.

Research in England demonstrates that a large proportion of people who murder are suicidal. Two people were executed in the United States in 1967. One was a person who hitch-hiked to Oklahoma where the death penalty was still in use. As soon as he crossed the state line, he killed the person who picked him up, stood there waiting to be apprehended. By the luck of the draw, he was appointed a public defender who was against the death penalty and got him life imprisonment. This guy was really ticked off.

He strangled his cellmate, said now you have to execute me, and they obliged him. After the US Supreme Court temporarily voided the death penalty nationwide in 1972 in *Furman* v. *Georgia*, people said, 'There's going to be a bloodbath, especially in the South.' The two states with the highest murder rates at the time were Georgia and Florida. In Georgia, the murder rate was 17.4 per 100,000 population, and in Florida it was 15.4. By 1977 when they executed Gary Gilmore, rates in both states they had dropped – in Georgia to 11.7, and in Florida to 10.2. After Florida executed John Spekelink, the murder rate went back up, which may have been because all the drugs had started coming into the country.

The reason we almost had the death penalty in New York is that a young cop, Ed Burns, was guarding the house of a witness in a drug case, and four guys came up and blew him away. So the legislators in New York who had previously opposed the death penalty, now voted for it. Jim Murphy, who is with the State Coalition for Criminal Justice, looked at some of the statistics.

Murphy looked at states from 1975 to 1985; states that had carried out executions, states that had death rows but no executions (like California, Ohio, and Pennsylvania), and states that had no death penalty at all. The highest rates of murder, both for police officers and members of the general public, were in states that executed. In fact, the general murder rate in executing states was actually double that in states with no death penalty at all. The same pattern continues.

People assume those sentenced to die have had fair trials. They do not look at what is going on. The new Supreme Court in California has recently ruled on several cases. In one, a man was convicted of murdering someone during a robbery and was sentenced to die. In sentencing him, the judge referred to his long violent criminal record as aggravating circumstances warranting the death penalty. Unfortunately, the judge was wrong; the man had no prior convictions. The judge died, the sentence was appealed, and the California Supreme Court ruled his error 'harmless.'

Next is the case of Richard William Garrison, convicted of two murders and a robbery, and sentenced to death in the gas chamber. His lawyer was an alcoholic who drank throughout the trial. In fact, he has since died of alcoholism. The Court stipulates that he drank in the morning, during the court recesses and throughout the evening. One day, when he was driving to the jury selection, he was arrested for drunk driving with a blood alcohol level of .270. Yet the Supreme Court found that Garrison had effective assistance of counsel.

Jeffrey Sheldon was convicted of first degree murder and kidnapping. During the penalty phase of the trial, the jury was told about a previous crime for which he had been prosecuted – the murder of a policeman. Evidence from that trial was admitted even though the man had been acquitted of the crime. The California Supreme Court ruled this to be an honest error.

You can go on in other jurisdictions. One guy was drunk and stayed overnight in jail. He was defending a woman and came back the next day without any preparation and continued with the defense. She was sentenced to death and is now on death row.

John Young, who was executed, was a kid whose single mother was prostituting herself to help support him. One night, when he was eight years old, she slept in the same bed with him. After several hours passed, someone came in and murdered his mother. John went to the streets to support himself. He was probably into prostitution, drugs, and all kinds of street crime. One day, when he was 19 and high on drugs, he went into a room of elderly people and killed four of them. If some of the survivors were called as witnesses, they would have asked that he not be executed. His lawyer gave no defense at all in the penalty phase of the trial. At the time of the trial, the lawyer had been drug addicted, was getting a divorce from his wife, was having fights with his homosexual lover and he was engaged in a child custody dispute. Soon after, he was disbarred, and wound up somewhere out in Washington or Oregon. Young's lawyers did not bother to raise the issue of ineffective counsel on appeal. Just before he was slated to die, a volunteer lawyer stepped in again took the case to the Supreme Court. They finally tracked down his trial lawyer 8-10 years later. He said I gave the defendant ineffective counsel because of A, B, C, D. William Rehnquist for the Supreme Court said it was untimely, sorry about that, off you go.

There have been several cases where the Supreme Court has ruled appeals untimely. When a justice has been missing in four-to-four decisions, the death sentence has always been upheld. Several people have been executed that way like Roosevelt Green, a young black kid with no prior record. He was hanging out on a street corner. His friend Moore comes along and says, 'Get in, we're going for a ride.' Green gets in. They drive to a little shop. Moore says, 'Come on in with me. I'm going to get something.' Roosevelt Green goes in, Moore pulls a gun, robs the place, and takes the young white woman clerk hostage. They leave. Moore gives Green the car keys and some money and says, 'Take my car up the road and fill it with gas.' While Green is gone, Moore kills the girl. For this, Roosevelt Green was executed, while Ardel Moore is still on death row. He has better lawyers. The judge even acknowledged that Green did not plan the murder, that he did not do it, and that he did not know it was going to happen. But according to law, if you participate in any way in the commission of a felony, you are as guilty as anyone.

There are four cases of men who were executed, who were not trigger men. Anthony Antone apparently carried a message from one group of people to another that resulted in the killing of a police officer. This made him part of the murder. He was sentenced to death because he would not fight it because he knew when he died his soul would go out the pituitary gland and out through the seven layers of the universe and bring him to the place from which he would rule the world.

I could give horror story after horror story. I could give you good reason to believe five people who have been executed since 1977 have been totally innocent. The latest was the case of Willie Darden, which gained international exposure. Willie was born to a 15-year-old-girl in Florida. When she was 17 she had another baby who died in childbirth. Willie was sort of passed around and in and out of foster care. Then he met up with another woman. He was about eighteen, they started living together, and she got pregnant. He was convicted once for taking something out of a mailbox. Next he forged a check for under $100 to buy food for his family. He was sentenced to 20 years. He got out in the mid 1960s after serving 16 years. He was driving on a two-lane road to pick up his wife to go to a wedding. A car pulled out to pass coming straight at him. He went into the ditch and could not get his car out. He went up to a white woman's house and asked her to call a tow truck at 5:30. Christine Welsh stayed with him until his car was pulled out of the ditch at about 6:00. Meanwhile, at 5:30, a half-hour drive away, a black man went into a shop and killed the owner in front of this man's wife. Another kid who went into the store to see what was going on got shot in the face, but lived. They showed mug shots of a lot of parolees to the woman. She said it was not Willie Darden. In the courtroom at trial, there was one black person – everyone else white – and she said, 'I can tell color, that's him.' The prosecutor said that this man should not have been allowed out of prison without a leash. Someone ought to shoot him in the face. His lawyer said he had never read such a prejudiced transcript. This case went to the Supreme Court at least three times. Every time it was turned down. Christine Welsh had gone to Darden's trial lawyer beforehand and said, 'I will testify that I was with him at the time.' She was never called. He was found guilty and sentenced to death. She asked the lawyer why she had not been called. The trial lawyer reported that the cops had changed the time of the crime to 6:00, and claimed that Garten had pulled out of the ditch at 5:30. Thus, he could have driven to the murder scene in time for the crime. Darden was sentenced to death. Every time he got an execution date, Christine Welsh went a little berserk. He had seven stays of execution before he was finally killed.

Christine Welsh worked at a hospital. She talked to the chaplain who said, 'Why don't you go see Sam Starks,' the minister called to the murder scene. So she tracked down Starks. He said he very clearly remembered the case. He told her, 'I was to meet with the head of my denomination that night at 6:30 about my change of parish so I was watching the time very closely. I was called at 25 minutes to 6:00 and left there at 5 minutes to 6:00 after having consoled the widow.' He signed an affidavit to this effect. This evidence went to the United States Supreme Court, who said, 'Too bad.' He was executed in March of 1988.

There is just one story after another like these. I have found that the most effective way to reach people is stories. All the statistics do not mean anything unless you can put a face on them and put a story to them.

The racism involved stands out. I have gone into inner-city schools where a lot of kids are in favor of the death penalty until you start telling stories and giving them the statistics. Like only 30 white people in the history of this country have ever been executed for killing blacks, or no white man has ever been executed for raping a black woman, and this sort of thing. Those kids sort of stop and think about it again. There are various ways of reaching people ....

3   On Culture and Abolition

Tony Nieto

My name is Tony Nieto, Apache Mescalaro Indian. And I come to you from California. The state of California. I am here for two purposes but mainly I want to share with you an experiences of my son, Angry Bear. Angry Bear was an Indian boy who learned the white man's law. It was because of his ability to help other prisoners – be they Blacks, Whites, Mexicans, or whatever – that the prison system murdered him. It was murder, cut-and-dried.

About a year before his murder, I visited him in San Quentin prison. He told me 'Dad, I'm not going to make it to the streets.' 'Why son?' I inquired. 'Is it the prison cliques, the gangs?' 'No dad,' he replied. 'I can deal with that. The prison administration is going to take me out.'

'But why would they do that son?,' I asked. 'It is because I have become a threat to them, dad.' I told him that I did not understand. 'Well dad, when I was in Soledad, I filed a writ of *habeas corpus* against the prison system of California for depriving the Indians of a sweat lodge. The federal law strictly states that American Indians cannot be imprisoned for any length of time without access to a sweat lodge. The sweat lodge is to the Indian what the church is to the white man. Now I'm suing San Quentin for forty thousand dollars because they took away my Indian religion, cultural artifacts, my photos, and my letters. They even took away the medication that was given to me by the prison medical staff.'

'Son, I can't help you,' I said, 'but they'd better not make a mistake.'

He smiled at me and replied, 'Yeah dad, I know cause you're a "takin' care of business" kind of dad.'

For a year I told my girlfriend, 'One of these days, I'm going to get a telegram saying my son is dead.' The day came. The telegram said that my son was shot through the chest and killed for failing to heed a warning shot as he was observed trying to stab another prisoner.

At first I was ready to accept the official version. After making arrangements to have his body sent home, I telephoned the prison. A female correctional officer answered the call. I told her that I wanted to speak to someone who might tell me what happened in the yard that morning. 'I am the father of the Indian prisoner that was killed.' She said, 'Well I can tell you what happened. Your son was shot through the chest and killed because he failed to heed a warning shot. He did accomplish his purpose , however.' I said, 'What purpose was that?' 'He stabbed another prisoner,' she said.

After 10 1/2 months of sobriety and attendance at AA meetings, I was really getting myself together. After hearing that news on the telephone, I went on a three-day drunk. The reason it lasted three days is because at the end of the third day I received a letter from my son's cellmate, the Indian brother George Walker. He wrote: 'Tony, the cowards shot him in the back. Don't let them get away with it.'

I am currently fighting the California prison system. I am suing the guard who killed my son. I am suing the warden of the prison, and I am suing the director of the entire California prison system.

The first article to appear in my hometown newspaper in Riverside described the incident exactly the way it had been described to me by the prison officials. It said that my son had been shot through the chest and killed for failing to heed a warning shot as he was observed trying to stab another inmate. Being an ex-convict myself, I know that they have no warning shot policy – signs everywhere in the prison attest to this – so how could my son fail to heed a warning-shot if there is no policy of warning shots? Prison officials told the *LA Times* that my son failed to heed a *verbal* warning. Can you see the difference? This incident is not over yet. I attended an inquiry at which the guard who killed my son said he gave no warning of any kind. There were two shots fired. Both were direct hits on my son, one in the back and one on the left biceps. The prison administration tried to cover it up.

They sent me interrogatories, two questions from which I shall share with you. The first, 'How much cost value do you put on the life of your son?' I answered with a lawsuit. I demanded a jury trial, when you answer to my lawsuit you demanded a jury trial, nothing's changed. Let the jurors decide what the cost value is; however, the bottom line is that my son's life is irreplaceable. My son was a professional guitarist, a song writer, artistic, a singer, a boxing champion in the prison system, he had a lot going for him – a lot for a twenty-six year old. They had the audacity to ask me, 'How much pain and suffering do you believe your son went through before he died?' 'Ask the correctional officer who shot my son,' I replied. The officer received his reward. Not even 6 months had elapsed since he killed my son before he was promoted to sergeant. He did his job. They used the prison investigation simply to report that 'No knives or contraband found in the yard.' If that were the case, how could my son have stabbed anyone?. Not long after, I received a copy of the report complete with a photograph of a male person. a report with a picture and in the picture there's a profile of a male. There is a hole in his chest and there is an arrow pointing to it marked 'entry wound.' There is also a hole in the left biceps. An arrow pointing to it is marked 'exit wound.' Despite this evidence, the gunner says that he shot my son in the left biceps so as to disable him – disable him from what? On the man's back in the photo, there is a tiny small hole with no stipulation as to entry or exit, just a small puncture wound. So they have marked the exit wound as an entry wound and they have marked the entry wound as an exit wound. They are lying, and I have trapped them in that lie.

They call this country the United States; however, there is nothing is united about it. The country is really in bad shape. There is no unity for anyone. No unity for the Indian, no unity for the black man, no unity for the white man, no unity for anyone. If there were such a thing as unity, then the brother, Little Rock Reed, and the brother, Geronimo Prep, would not be imprisoned because they refuse to walk out into the free world carrying the stipulations of parole with which they have been burdened.

I would also like to share with you news about the new model prison for this country that has been built in California. We're always first aren't we? The governor of California took measure, and built Pelican Bay State Prison, a throw back to the Medieval period. The prisoners in these places live in a Security Housing Unit (SHU) made up of little cells constructed out of concrete. There's a steel door that has 2-inch-round holes in it. Twenty-two-and-a-half hours a day are spent in that tiny cell.

If the prisoner wants to shower, he must first be humiliated by a strip search. After showering, the prisoner is forcefully subjected to another strip search. If the prisoner wants to go to the yard - referred to as the "dog run," – he will find himself in just a tiny yard surrounded by 18 foot walls. There is neither sunshine nor equipment for working out. There is just the prisoner and the yard.

As far as the extraction team goes, they do a job on you – a good job. A month-and-a-half after they killed Angry Bear, I had another son in the same prison. The prison workers told him, 'Your father's a damn liar. We didn't shoot your brother in the back. Here are the pictures.' They only showed him the pictures of Angry Bear from the front, apparently shot through the chest. 'How much does your father know?' My second son replied, 'In answer to your first statement, my father's not a liar. In answer to your second question, my father knows enough to take you people down to the dirt and knowing my father, he's going to do that.' They beat him up – badly – and I have the pictures to prove it. They gassed him, beat him up, stood him in a hot car, and sent him to another prison where he was immediately segregated in the 'hole.' I called the FBI who took 35 days to find him. Mind you, he's in a state prison, and it still took 35 days for them to find him. I have a letter from the FBI stating 'blah blah blah blah blah ... not enough prosecution merit, we're closing the case. Thank you for letting us be of service to you.' I now have four of those letters. One letter concerns the time the that they beat Angry Bear in Soledad. Another letter concerns the time they beat up Angry Bear in Tahachi. The third letter is from when they killed Angry Bear. I sent them evidence, I sent them clippings, and they sent me a letter which said 'not enough prosecution merit, we're closing the case. Thank you for letting us be of service to you.' The final letter is the one concerning the beating of my second son – we talk of justice.

Well, I can tell you that justice *will* be served, and not because I am going to settle this case – there will be no settlement. My son's life was not and is not for sale. I am going to take those people to the box. The gunner, the warden, and the director of the whole California prison system. I have been approached by movie agents make a film. I've been talking to Kevin Costner's father who lives about fifteen miles from me. At this time channel 28 in California is talking to *60 Minutes* about putting me on. People ask, 'Aren't you afraid that the system is going to take you out?' Excuse me, I'm 58 years old. It makes no difference to me what the system does. They' are welcome to take me out, if that is what they must do; however, they will not be taking me out, at least not until the grandfather's promise comes to pass. 'Not one hair of my head will be touched until I fulfill the purpose that he put me here for.' Thank you very much.

Lionel White Bird

I want to thank our brother who has shared with us the story of his son's murder. Sitting and listening to that story brings out my anger to a degree. My name is Lionel White Bird. I am a Plains Cree Indian from Rejackasas, Saskatchewan, but I now reside in Ontario where I am involved with the Canadian prison system.

I went into the Canadian federal prison system in 1979 and was released in 1984/85. I just became a free citizen in Canada, February of 1989. I restructured my priorities. I put that drug and alcohol spirit (as I call it) away. In looking for a better way, I began seeking out the elders, the traditional people. I began to think about going back to that prison system in order to help my brothers and sisters. Through Grandfather Creator, today I am back in a place that I once hated with all my heart.

In the prison for women there are many suicides. Most of the women there are native women from Saskatchewan. The hardest thing for me to do is go and tell one of them that her older brother shot her younger brother. Through all the suicides, as an ex-offender I am thankful I have access to that prison. I am thankful to be able to visit the segregation area, to visit the prison hospital, to assist them in wiping out their rage. I am thankful to Grandfather Creator. Today I sit in on meetings at the regional head office, and they are asking me for my advice about the Canadian penitentiary system – me, an ex-offender, someone they always wanted to throw in the hole and beat up on in prison. Just like you Americans, we Canadian abolitionists will run into many obstacles. If we want to bring someone in to do the sweat, they have to be checked out by security. They create problems, real hurdles. To get the drums into one of the institutions we have to write a proposal. We have to go through all this, and then they are going to build a sound-proof room. I said no, you do not take that heartbeat into a sound-proof room.

It is good to be at this, my first, abolition conference. Through Art Solomon, a couple months ago I said I would try to come down here to Bloomington. In Canada we just came from a national liaison conference in Edmonton, Alberta, of representative delegates from each province, all the native people who work from the West to East coast of Canada. We basically tried to do the same thing as here. I have to be truthful about that conference. I told Art that, to a degree, I was a little bit annoyed by it because, in Kingston as at the one before, it seemed like everyone addressed the issues and exchanged views, but no one talked about what we were going to do. It was like we will set a date for the next conference and we will see you all there next year. And guess what happened? We talked about the same things this year. The one thing I was happy to see in Kingston was that they gave the ex-offenders a voice. Correctional Services of Canada were there for the first time. They had to sit down and listen to us where before it was the other way around. It was good, but at Edmonton, for some reason, we were not given a chance to speak.

I am proud to be part of this conference and to be given the opportunity to speak. The struggle is long and hard, and many times when I leave prison, I leave in anger. Many times when I come out of the women's penitentiary I have to put tobacco down, and I say Grandfather, why? My sisters are killing themselves here. They are going home in body bags. We just finished having a riot there. Most involved were native women. I go down to segregation and I see them crying, they're hurting. We have the women elders, the women traditional teachers come in. Kingston is not very big but there is only a handful of us and we cannot cover all of the institution. I am thankful that I have the right to go into a lot of the prisons and talk the men and the women. There is a lot of suffering. I am thankful that the lodge is there, that the pipe is there, that those elders are there. I do not call myself a spiritual advisor because I am still at a stage of learning, but I share what I can. I tell them that together we can find an answer, together we can make that circle strong. And when the miracle happens, we make it happen together. I am in that very process right now. So it is good to be here and listen to our brothers and sisters who are involved with the American prisons down here. Maybe I can take back some of their ideas in terms of helping our brothers and sisters in the Canadian penitentiary system up there.

Achebe Lateef

I am an ex-prisoner and I speak for a lot of people still locked down in the prisons. On behalf of the African National Prisoner Organization primarily and CURE (Citizens United to Rehabilitate Errants), I really appreciate the opportunity to address an international audience about some of our issues. Though the audience here may be small, it is an international grouping right here, and our taped message may, I hope, go out all over.

We think it was appropriate that the Native Americans opened this session because we whole heartedly believe as Africans that North America actually belongs to the Native American people, that the US Government is illegal, illegally occupying this territory. It may not come across in our everyday dealings with one another, but there are large groups of Africans in this country, born in America, who actually feel this way. We understand the nature of colonialism, and when we gather internationally, we should recognize that the term colonialism has international significance. I think that everyone who is sitting here recognizes that. We recognize that the Native people in America, North American and African people in North America, are still living in colonial bondage. As many of you probably know, next year there will be a celebration. They are calling it the Columbus Celebration and we are calling the celebration 500 years of genocide. When they say that Columbus discovered America, we say he brought genocide right onto North American shores. A lot of people do not like to hear us say that. We do not care about that though. We are going to say it because that is what the situation is.

We also say that the spirit of Angry Bear lives. His father showed that this morning. We want to support his father because we understand what struggle is. There is plenty of struggle going on right here in Indiana. When you come to our workshop tomorrow morning we will tell you about a lot that is going on right here in Indiana. Political prisoners and prisoners of war are being held right here in Indiana on Indiana death row.

We also second the Native American brother's assertion that this is not the United States. People on the inside call it the United Snakes of America, and with good reason. The United Snakes of America. As you probably know from all of the history of the Native American people, even from the popular culture from TV, that the native people have always said that the Europeans spoke with what? A forked tongue, like the snake's tongue. We were also glad that the native people mentioned some of our freedom fighters like Geronimo Pratt who is locked down right now in a California prison.

The four letters that Tony got from the FBI about Angry Bear are typical. In this country we have always believed that the FBI was in fact the Ku Klux Klan. Anybody who has kept up with the history of the FBI, as in the 'Eyes on the Prize' video on public TV, or COINTELPRO documents obtained through the Freedom of Information Act, has found that during the civil rights era, every time someone was killed and a Klansman was accused of it, the Ku Klux Klansman turned out to be an informant for the FBI. The FBI is the Klan. A lot of people do not want to hear that, but we will keep on saying it to support a kind of insurgency we believe is going on right here in North America.

Our insurgent movement began when we came over here in chains, and when the Native people began to be treated with tremendous disrespect, and to have genocide committed on them. We will keep on talking about insurgency, we know why the head of the Department of Corrections here in Indiana is not attending these sessions. He would have to come face-to-face with the wrath of the people, including me, a member of the African National Prisoner Organization, an ex-prisoner from maximum security, now a prisoner out here in minimum security.

I know what I am talking about. I spent twelve-and-a-half years right here in Indiana prisons. Twelve-and-a-half years. I have been out of prison now for almost five years. I am the one you never hear about. The ones that you do hear about are the ones who got out of prison and went back, the ones who get out of prisons and kill somebody. There are plenty of ex-prisoners like me out here now, engaged in community activism. Prison officials do not want to see us coming, the prisons are glad that we are gone. They say Governor, Mayor, Police Chief, you can deal with them now, we ain't going to make deals with them no more.

We managed to survive and make it back out here to the outside, and we are glad we can address this international body. The statistic that has been going around the country lately, that one out of four African men is tied to the prison system, is a statistic that the African National Prisoner Organization has been putting out since 1979. Since 1979! I have a couple of old journals here that I will share with you later on. We call it the criminal injustice system, thanks to *Instead of Prisons* (1976) by Fay Honey Knopp who is sitting right over here right now on my left. She taught us when we read that book several years ago. We were leading a lot of prison struggles about dishonest and honest language about the problems we face. We would like to thank her for giving us the courage to talk about 'penitentiaries' rather than 'correctional facilities.' We call ourselves prisoners and not inmates, we call correctional officers guards and turnkeys because that is what they are. We found out that honest language helps to empower you. If your language is not honest, if your language is confusing, then you are not going to solve the problem. But what comes out of honest language is that there has to come some honest practice.

Another problem we have faced is getting inside the prisons. We have not been able to get inside of the prisons because of what we represented when we were in the prisons: the transformation of the colonial criminal mentality. Everybody asks us now, 'What can we do about the prisons?' We keep saying, if you just want to know what you can do about the prisons you will never be able to solve the problem. It did not start in prison. It started out here in society. We became criminal out here in society. The colonial mentality is out here. You cannot look at prison in isolation from the rest of society, if you are going to talk about solving the problem.

Once in prison, we want to transform the colonial criminal mentality into a revolutionary mentality. We do not talk about revolution here in this country enough. Particularly in prisons, you get problems when you talk about revolution. But the only thing that is going to change that criminal mentality, that colonial mentality, is a revolutionary mentality. When people ask, 'What can you do to change criminal behavior?' you must go to the source of the problem and you must tell the truth. Problems stem strictly from the fact that the African's identity was stolen, and the Native people's cultures were taken when they were put on reservations. What we have here in this mixture we call the United Snakes of America is white male domination, white supremacy. We will continue to go around in circles until we address these core truths, unless we deal with them honestly. We always tell anyone who listens to us, even today. Though as opposed to 25 years ago, Africans have over 7,000 elected black officials and no telling how many of the Toms the Native people have in the Bureau of Indian Affairs, the conditions of our people are getting worse and worse and worse. Go back and read the Kerner Commission (1970) on the violence in this country 20 around years ago, and it will tell you the system has not changed. The neighborhoods are colonies, they are all doing without, there is not enough work to go around, so what happened? what happened! We say neo-colonialism. That is what happened. The strategy became neo-colonialism.

Everybody wants to know where the gangs are coming from. We say that the government put them in place with a counter-insurgency program when they killed the freedom movement off back in the 1960s. The gangs started out there in south-central Los Angeles County, in California, the home of Ronald Reagan, and Attorney General Ed Meese who subsequently became President and Attorney General respectively of this country as a reward. Just as Tony told us, the guard who killed his son was promoted six months later. Right here in Indiana, John Nunn became second in command of the Department of Correction after he signed off on letting a man out who everybody in the world knew wanted to kill his wife as soon as he could get to her, Alan Matheney. When they elevated Nunn, they shut down work release and slammed the door on everyone in prison. There are people now who would have been out of prison a long time ago, had it not been for John Nunn.

Alan Matheney is on death row right now. We are opposed to the death penalty, but if anyone ought to be sitting on death row right now with Alan Matheney, it is John Nunn: a boot licking, neo-colonial, African man right here in this state, second-in-command of the Department of Corrections for Indiana. We think, Indiana Commissioner of Corrections, Jim Aiken, did not want to show up here because he knew he was going to get hit in the face with this.

I have heard some people say earlier that people here are going to come up with concrete plans for activism. I just found out about this conference this year, I did not know that they had ICOPA one, two, three and four. The one thing I think we can accomplish, whether we go out of here with marching orders and banners and clipboards, is that this conference can be a voice. If we can begin to understand conceptually where the real crime comes from and who the real criminals are, then we can begin to patch this hole that we have in our social tire. Right now we have a continual slow leak, because we keep thinking that there will be more legislators here, or we need more money over there, or we need to have more people, or we need to invent alternatives. That is not the situation. I, as a victim, continually sit with the suit-and-tie people to explain what the situation is, but they do not want to hear it. Just now the Governor's wife in this state is going around saying that they are going to be able to gauge how many prison cells they will need in the future by the at-risk second graders. She is talking about seven-year-old kids without any social consciousness whatsoever; but, they are planning cells for them. 'At-risk' means that the mother is working two jobs somewhere, daddy is probably already in the penitentiary somewhere, there are 3 or 4 kids in the house or somewhere unknown, and the police have already picked up the kid a few times. Instead of understanding what that situation is, what is going on, we are supposed to plan how many cells we are going to need, and to spend from 15, 000 to 30,000 dollars, depending on what part of the country you are in, to keep a person for a year. While the family the prisoners come from manage only to make $8,000 a year, or $12,000 at best, before taxes. This new model prison they have out there in California, with the cells Tony talked about, that is what they are going to do. Those are the priorities of the United States government and its local agencies. That is what is going on in this country. We are hoping this ICOPA V will be able to give an international voice to these concerns, particularly of those of us here in Indiana and in the prisons and in the lock up units and on the death rows who do not have a voice any other way.

4   On Radical Feminism and Abolition

Fay Honey Knopp

Many people who know of my involvement in helping to produce *Instead of Prisons* have asked me: 'How come you shifted from abolition to sexual-abuse issues?' There is no shift. The issue of sexual abuse and how society responds to and punishes it is an abolitionist issue. Similarly, this morning's presentations by our Native brothers and sisters are also part of the response that needs to be included if we are going to have a truly abolitionist perspective. The issues for people of color and feminist issues are inclusive not separate tracts.

One of the things that I wanted to do after helping to write *Instead of Prisons* was to look at one of what could be considered the more serious behaviors. I wanted to look at sexual offences in depth in terms of their effect, of the roots in social structure, and of more global issues. I wanted to begin with issues of primary prevention, look at how society is responding to these issues, and try to find out something that we could do, hands on, to reduce the harm done both to victim/survivors and to offenders, and how we can prevent those.

Since 1976, we[1] have undertaken studies on sexual offense issues and the way we have done that was to deal directly with the people involved. From my perspective, this is the only way of doing any kind of research or trying to formulate some kind of response that will not do more harm to people. We have traveled around the country, visited most of the offender treatment programs, and visited and worked with most of the victim/survivor programs. We have tried to lay out what some notions of restorative justice (what I call an abolitionist perspective) are and might be when dealing with sexual abuse. In the excerpt that follows, I outline what the key elements to such a position are.[2]

In the United States, public perceptions of crimes and justice come from a variety of sources. Some views are rooted authentically in personal experiences; but, for a majority of people, beliefs about crimes and justice are shaped by a constant bombardment of the media's portrayal of crimes and criminals, by office seekers who exploit fear as a political issue, and by a very well-funded law-enforcement apparatus.

Getting our primary views on justice from such biased sources as the media and law enforcement is comparable to having our perceptions of war, peace, and foreign policy shaped by the Pentagon and its generals. The view we are given is, in fact, a *war model:* persons who commit crimes are seen as the 'enemy in our midst,' and solutions offered are more punishments, more weapons, more caging of human beings. But war-model responses to problems that are essentially social, cultural, political, and economic have failed and will continue to fail.

One reason war model responses fail is because they neglect victim-survivors, leaving them outside the criminal *injustice* process. Victims' needs are not placed at the center of the process; rather, victims most often are used by the prosecution for their own adversarial purposes. Not only is the victim the forgotten person in the process, but, in cases involving sexual victimization the victim is usually the one who is blamed, the victim is the one who is on trial, the victim is the one who must prove that victimization has occurred.

We also know that these war-model responses have failed because offenders' needs for restoration, resocialization, and re-education are rarely considered in the sentencing process. Caging the offender is accepted most often as the 'just' response to the commission of a sexual crime; the length of prison punishment is equated with the amount of 'justice' to be done.

Prisons *do not work.* They do not reduce crimes; they do not rehabilitate people; they rarely deter; and they fail to protect the public in any enduring way. Imprisonment punishes deeply and expensively in both human and fiscal costs, with damaging effects to both the individual and the community. Prisons punish mainly the poor, the minorities, the powerless, the 'losers,' the young. Increasingly, prisons are being used to punish women, and to punish them more harshly than ever before.

In states where sex-offender retraining programs are available (see Knopp 1984), judges are provided an option for sentencing sex offenders to a program offering an opportunity for a lifestyle change. Where alternatives are not available, neither judges, offenders, nor the community are offered options other than the prison or the asylum. Without appropriate alternatives, the caging mentality takes over. In the United States, we have more people imprisoned than ever before,[3] and the number of cages on the drawing boards is expanding beyond all expectations. Such unparalleled expansion only reinforces the war-model belief that more prisons somehow will provide a solution to violent and sexually violent behaviors. As long as the nonsolution of imprisonment is relied upon, the public is relieved of having to make connections between the root causes of antisocial and sexually violent acts and the kind of social-change alternatives that actually could make our communities more just and safe. As long as we use imprisonment as the primary response to sexual crimes, the majority of people can hold on to their mistaken beliefs that there are 'criminal types' and 'bad seeds' and biological imperatives for people to behave this way.

As long as the primary feminist response to the crime of rape, for instance, is to demand longer, harsher sentences for rapists, we inhibit ourselves from addressing the roots of this behavior. Until we as feminists have a coherent, well-articulated, well-thought analysis to counter the war-model response to criminal sexual behaviors – behaviors that not only are socially and culturally learned, but in fact are supported and perpetuated by societal institutions and practices – we will foster an increasingly caged and punitive society.

In *Instead of Prisons* (Knopp et al. 1976: 150), we reprinted a feminist editorial that said in part:

> If all men who had ever raped were incarcerated tomorrow, rape would continue outside as well as inside prisons. Incarceration does not change the societal attitudes that promote rape. In a society that deals with symptoms rather than causes of problems, prisons make perfect sense. Confronting the causes of rape would threaten the basic structure of society...Prison is vindictive – it is not concerned with change but with punishment. And its real social function is similar to that of rape – it acts as a buffer,

as an oppressive institution where a few scapegoats pay for the ills of society.(MacMillan and Klein 1974)

Mutual education/action strategies on feminist and abolitionist agendas will contribute significantly to a safer and more just society. We will be expending our energies toward controlling and reducing sexual aggression and violence rather than reinforcing and strengthening already extremely oppressive structures.

Prison abolition perspectives are set forth in *Instead of Prisons*. This abolitionist publication was designed originally to offer a conceptual foundation and action strategies for facilitating the gradual process of reducing imprisonment while building up a variety of nonrepressive alternatives. One of our tasks was to learn good methods for teaching these concepts and becoming involved in the first step of the social-change process,[4] which is *consciousness raising* – 'seeing the need for the new.' In this case, the perceived need is for a new system of restorative justice based on social and economic justice and on concern and respect for all victims and victimizers, a new system based on remedies and restoration rather than on prison punishment and victim neglect, a new system rooted in the concept of a caring community.

Although people need to conceptualize their own visions of a caring community, The Safer Society Program defines it as a place where 'power and equality of all social primary goods – liberty, opportunity, income, wealth, and the bases of self-respect – are institutionally structured and distributed to all members of the community and where the spirit of reconciliation prevails' (Knopp et al. 1976: 10). The Safer Society books, manuals, and workshops help to raise this kind of consciousness. Our primary message is that the sources of antisocial behavior are rooted in the social, political, cultural, and economic structures of society and that solutions must be found there. That does not imply either that persons are not responsible for their behaviors or that we do nothing until the caring community is a reality. It does imply that safer and more just social strategies flow from a social-change agenda advocating social responsibility rather than the traditional crime-prevention/war-model agenda.

If the first step of social change is consciousness raising or seeing the need for the new, the second step is *creativity* or learning how to organize and construct the new. In our case, this means creating a new restorative-justice model in crimes of sexual aggression and violence.

It is extremely difficult to conceptualize a new restorative-justice model when we are dealing with issues of sexual violence. I know this from my own experience. Sexual victimizations make me raging mad. I feel angry, injured, and often vengeful when I listen to the horrendous cases of child and adult sexual abuse that come across our phone and through the mail, or occur in my neighborhood. I try to acknowledge and deal with my anger and then redirect it toward creating a new concept of justice and changing the social conditions that encourage and promote sexual aggression.

In trying to put theories of creativity into practice, many of us in the movement to control sexual abuse are encouraging communities to identify and deal with its root causes. We are moving victim services and offender treatment into a comprehensive perpetrator-prevention framework and forming networks to carry on this work. We are advocating corrective legislation. We are identifying which sexually aggressive behaviors can be handled in the community and which require a controlled environment, and we are trying to implement these and other comprehensive services for both victim/survivors and offenders.

The pressure is always excessive for abolitionists to produce a *plan*, a plan that solves every problem and deals with every criminal act before abolition can be considered. But it is not necessary to have a finished blueprint; it is not necessary to know the last step before taking the first step. The first step towards abolition is to break with the old system and help conceptualize the new.[5]

Though there is no blueprint for abolition, The Safer Society Program offers an 'Attrition Model' (ibid.: 62-63) for gradually wearing away the use of imprisonment and simultaneously building a caring community. There are four dynamically interrelated strategies to be pursued, some of which present challenge areas for feminist/abolitionists to consider.

The first strategy is to stop the growth of the prison system, to say 'no' to building any more cages. This is called the *moratorium* strategy (ibid.: 64-80).

The second, called the *decarceration* strategy (ibid.: 81-98), is an attempt to get people who are already inside out of jail or prison. For instance, the abolition of bail in the United States would release at least 50 to 60 percent of the jail population. For those involved in issues of sexual violence, community safety, and constitutional liberties, this presents a challenge: Should persons who have been accused and/or have prior histories of sexually violent behaviors, and who have not yet been found guilty, be released to the community before trial? Should they be released with conditions restricting their movement? If so, should such restrictions be enforced? These issues of community safety and preventive detention of sex offenders are serious constitutional- and safety-challenge areas we need to address in our mutual agendas.

A third strategy is one of excarceration, which involves moving away from the notion of imprisonment (ibid.: 99-127). There are hundreds of workable and appropriate examples of alternatives in practice currently. They include restitution, fines, community-service work, and dispute and mediation processes. Abolitionists support models of dispute mediation where the conflicting parties and members of their neighborhoods are trained to settle their low- and medium-level conflicts to the advantage of all disputants. Such processes do not determine guilt but determine responsibility for the behavior and how that responsibility will be played out to the satisfaction of the conflicting parties.[6] Clarity does not exist on the limitations of this type of alternative to the court and sentencing processes. Therein lies another challenge area. The National Center on Women and Family Law and other groups contend that dispute resolution, as it is presently practiced, is not beneficial to women in settling any problems involving family violence. They contend it has proved an inappropriate format for these reasons: (1) in such situations women do not have equal bargaining power; (2) few mediators are neutral; (3) mediation does not address or punish past behavior; and (4) communication with mediators often is not confidential.[7]

Seekers of a new justice are challenged: (1) to examine current models of dispute resolution; (2) in consort with the critics of these procedures, to try to determine when and if any type of family violence may be dealt with appropriately through such alternative procedures; and (3) where possible, together to try to construct a just model that can serve fairly all parties involved in family abuse. Proponents of dispute/mediation models should heed the advice of those directly affected and involved in such serious abuses.

The fourth strategy of the Attrition Model is called *restraint of the few*, and it addresses the concerns of feminists and abolitionists more than any of the other strategies. While there is little doubt that the majority of persons now imprisoned could remain in the community if an adequate continuum of alternatives were in place, some persons' behaviors would still present a real threat to public and personal safety. What alternatives, for instance, should abolitionists suggest for persons who have been convicted of very serious sexual crimes? The Safer Society Program focuses energy on this issue because we consider sexual offenses and family violence to be two of the most serious, most neglected, but also the most accepted categories of violent behavior.

In the postconviction phase, The Safer Society Program advocates competent and specialized assessment and evaluation of the sex offender. If the offender chooses the option of re-education and re-training and is considered a good candidate, we advocate residential treatment options. We most strongly advocate early remedial intervention with adolescents at the first demonstration of sexual aggression (Knopp 1982, 1985).

The principles undergirding The Safer Society Program's abolitionist perspectives on the restraint of persons who present a threat to personal and public safety are (1) that public safety and constitutional rights of victims and offenders be the overriding guiding principles, and (2) that the least restrictive and most humane option for the shortest period of time in the most remedial and restorative environment be applied.

Since 1975, in an effort to understand the issues involved in sexual offenses and to learn how to construct a new restorative justice, I have personally visited hundreds of community-based and residential programs for sex offenders. We have published criteria for assessing risk for community or residential treatment, along with the first study of adolescent sex offenders and their treatment (Knopp 1982). We have published a study of a range of community-based and residential programs that re-educate and re-train adult sex offenders (Knopp 1984). We are continually advocating and assisting treatment programs for sex offenders as a Safer Society strategy and publishing self-help manuals (Freeman-Longo 1988; Bay and Freeman-Longo 1989; Bays, Freeman-Longo, and Hildebran 1990). We are fostering perpetrator prevention strategies for all ages – the young to the elderly. These projects are the logical extension of our abolitionist commitment:

> As abolitionists we are confronted with the struggle between the conflicting forces for change. We are in total agreement with feminist anti-rape workers and other social changers that every effort should be made to apprehend and confront the sexually violent. We share the feelings of outrage experienced by rape victims; we believe that repetitive rapists must be restrained from committing further acts of violence. On the

other hand we do not support the response of imprisonment. We challenge the basic assumption that punishment, harsh sentences, and retributive attitudes will serve to lessen victims' pain, re-educate rapists, or genuinely protect society. Not all sex offenders must be restrained during their re-education/re-socialization process. But for those sexual violents who do require temporary separation from society – repetitive rapists, those who physically brutalize or psychologically terrorize and men who repeatedly assault children – places of restraint are needed while re-education occurs. Unless these alternatives are developed, there may be no other choice but the prison or the asylum. Hence the urgency for abolitionists to create programs similar to those we shall cite. (Knopp et al. 1976: 150-51)

Instead of Prisons, by working on behalf of victims, offenders, and a safer society committed to primary prevention of sexual abuse, we hope that we are *building a more caring community*, the all-encompassing strategy of the Attrition Model.

NOTES

1 The Safer Society Program, a national program of the New York State Council of Churches, formerly operated as the Prison Research/ Education/Action Project (PREAP).

2 What follows is exceprted from Honey Knopp (1991), with the kind permission of Indiana University Press.

3 Our best guess at ICOPA VI in San José, Costa Rica, June 2-5, 1993 was that, by then, there were 810 prisoners per 100,000 US inhabitants sitting in jail, prison, or juvenile detention – over 2million prisoners (eds.).

4 Four steps are identified in the social change process: (1) consciousness raising; (2) creativity; (3) structural continuity for distributing justice; and (4) second-wave consciousness-raising to keep the new system from becoming old, closed, and unchallenged. This process is based in part on concepts advanced by Manfred Halpern, Princeton University.

5 See also Mathieson 1974: 24-25.

6 Dispute mediation differs from arbitration where disputants give a third party legal authority to render a decision binding.

7 The National Center on Women and Family Law, 799 Broadway, Room 402, New York, NY 10003. Also see 'Violence in the Family,' *JSAC Grapevine*, January, 1987, vol. 18, no. 6 (Joint Strategy and Action Committee, Inc., 475 Riverside Drive, New York, NY 10115).

REFERENCES

Bays, L., and R. Freeman-Longo. 1989. *Why Did I do it Again?* Orwell, Vt: Safer Society Program

Bays, L., R. Freeman-Longo, and D. Hildebran. 1990. *How Can I Stop?* Orwell, Vt: Safer Society Program

Freeman-Longo, R., and L. Bays. 1988. *Who Am I and Why Am I in Treatment?* Orwell, Vt: Safer Society Program

Knopp, F., et al. 1976. *Instead of Prisons: A Handbook for Abolitionists.* Orwell, Vt: Safer Society Press

Knopp, F. 1982. *Remedial Intervention in Adolescent Sex Offenses: Nine Program Descriptions.* Orwell, Vt: Safer Society Press

– 1984. *Retraining Adult Sex Offenders: Methods and Models.* Orwell, Vt: Safer Society Press

– 1985. *The Youthful Sex Offender: The Rationale and Goals of Early Intervention and Treatment.* Orwell, Vt: Safer Society Press

MacMillan, J., and F. Klein. 1974. *Feminist Alliance Against Rape Newsletter*, September-October

Mathieson, T. 1974. *The Politics of Abolition.* New York: John Wiley and Sons

5 *Dading*: A Civil Law Alternative to the Dutch Penal System

Gert Jan Slump

Mieke Emmen

The Initiative

From December 1989 until December 1990, an experiment on a civil law alternative to penal prosecution took place in Amsterdam. The experiment, Project Strafrechtelijke Dading, was supervised by Humanitas, a National Union for Social Services and Community Development. The experiment was subsidized by the Dutch Department of Justice, the Dutch Probation Office (Nederlandse Federatie van Reklasseringsinstellingen), the Foundations on Probation (Stichtingen Reklassering) in Haarlem and Amsterdam, and a charitable fund (Koningin Juliana Fonds).

In Dutch civil law, a *dading* is an agreement by which parties finish a pending lawsuit or prevent a future lawsuit on handing over, promise, or retention of a matter. This agreement is only valid if concluded in writing (*Dutch Civil Code* art. 1888). The aim of the project was to investigate where agreements providing compensation or promises of future conduct could satisfy victims as much as criminal prosecution.

The option of negotiating a *dading* was offered to complainants and suspects in 208 randomly selected police magistrate cases.[1] Either party could terminate negotiations or initiate binding arbitration at any time. The Public Prosecutor promised not to prosecute in cases in which parties negotiated or had arbitrated a contract.

The contract cleared the case for the Public Prosecutor and offered the victim the basis for a civil-law recovery in the case of a non-fulfillment by the suspect of his or her obligations. Non-fulfillment did not have any penal-law repercussions. Parties either paid legal expenses or qualified for free legal services, and so the program paid for itself.

The program operated under social constraints:

- Only criminal cases already filed by the Public Prosecutor qualified for inclusion in the experiment to make this a true experiment. It was also expressed in the fact that once an agreement was concluded, prosecution was withdrawn with prejudice, so that the matter became purely civil.

- Agreement to a *dading* was entirely voluntary, and agreement had to be fully informed by two letters and comprehensive verbal instructions (see the 'practice').

- Project facilitators had to remain strictly neutral, and either party could retain legal counsel.

- Only minor cases falling under summary jurisdiction of police magistrates were eligible for participation (*snefrecht*).

- The Public Prosecutor reserved the right to exclude specific cases and cases of severe disturbance of the public order.

- An agreement had to be reached within two months (which after some time was extended to two-and-a-half months).

- The experiment had to be evaluated by the Research and Documentation Center of the Department of Justice of the Dutch Government.

- Confidentiality of personal written and oral data was maintained.

- The committee designing the experiment explicitly refused to call it a 'mediation' project. Rather, the experiment was rooted in a civil procedure which leaves initiative in the hands of the parties themselves. The Committee feared that 'mediators' might be inclined to take formulation and enforcement of the contract out of the hands of the parties themselves. This was to be an experiment in parties to conflict creating their own 'justice.'

- Contracts stipulated compensation for damage and liquidated damages for failure to perform an obligation which could be non-monetary, like 'street-interdiction' or 'shop-interdiction.'

- All cases were selected from one unit of the Public Prosecutor's Office covering most parts of Amsterdam, except the northern part and the center. In most cases the offense was alleged to have occurred from 6 to 12 months before selection into the experiment.

– In our random sample most cases concerned offenses against property (approximately 60 percent); in 32 percent of the cases, offenses against persons were charged.

The Background

The committee initiating the experiment presuming that a civil-law approach would be supposedly more complete, cheaper and faster than a penal law 'solution,' and less 'difficult' for both parties.

The civil law approach would be more *complete*, because the victim could be compensated in many more ways than is possible under Dutch penal law. Compensation by means of penal law is only possible in a restricted number of cases, and even in those cases, there are restricted monetary damages with a certain maximum. In civil law, parties themselves can agree to any lawful terms.

Some suggest the *dading* could be a criminal procedure, but the committee sought to avoid the possibility of tacking criminal penalties onto contracts. *Dadings* would be substantially cheaper than prosecution because court costs would only be incurred in cases of appeal from non compliance with the contract. Generally, a contract could be negotiated faster than the magistrate's court could dispose of the case. Victims could get right down to obtaining compensation instead of being distracted by penal issues. Besides, in Dutch jurisprudence, penal law is formally regarded as *'ultimum remedium,'* a last resort when other remedies have failed.

In sum, parties could get what they themselves wanted without the penal system doing any damage to either of them. The victim could play a much more active role in settling compensation than is possible in the Dutch penal process, because alleged offenders need not be afforded as much protection when the complainant is a single person rather than the state.

The Procedure

The experiment was administered by a Project Bureau of three persons. One person was charged with secretarial tasks, among them weekly selection of cases from the Public Prosecutor's Office. Excess cases were selected as 'shadow files' so that the Public Prosecutor would not know which cases were returned to him because parties had declined to negotiate or failed to reach agreement.

The other two Bureau-members were charged with contacting suspects, victims, and their lawyers, as well as with supporting the mutual communication between lawyers and between lawyers and their clients.

The first contact, both with suspect and victim, was a letter by the Public Prosecutor, which offered the option of negotiations and announced a forthcoming letter from the Project Bureau. The letter from the Project Bureau, sent two days later, contained a request that each party make an appointment for further information. If the suspect or victim concerned did not react within a week after the letter from the Project Bureau was sent, one of the Bureau members attempted to make contact by telephone or scheduled a visit; 83 percent of the suspects and 97 percent of the victims were thus contacted. In the randomly selected cases, the suspect was contacted first. If the suspect expressed willingness to negotiate with the victim, the victim was contacted.

On initial contact a conversation followed, the Project worker detailed information on the possibilities of negotiation, stressed the voluntary nature of participation, and gave the prospect of non-prosecution, even when an agreement incriminated the suspect. The resources available through the Project, including arrangement of legal assistance, were described.

Possibilities stressed to both victim and suspect were:

- Availability of binding arbitration in cases of irreconcilable disagreements;

- Notarial certification of the contract (especially stressed to complainants who doubted suspect compliance);

- The possibility of earning money by way of employment; an employment agency (Randstad) in Amsterdam was prepared to intercede to provide paid work;

- The possibility of a loan from the Municipal Credit Bank Amsterdam (Gemeentelijke Kredietbank Amsterdam);

- The possibility of a lien on monthly social welfare benefit payments enforced by the Municipal Social Security Office (Gemeentelijke Sociale Dienst);

– The possibility of referral for further victim support by the Probation Office; and

– The possibility of appraisal of damages in case of disagreement. In the conversations, 78.6 percent of the suspects and 82 percent of the victims reached made clear that they were prepared to negotiate.

When one party was prepared to negotiate, a lawyer was contacted as soon as possible for those who did not already have one. A pool of 22 lawyers in Amsterdam was formed, most of them so-called 'social lawyers.' They were thoroughly informed on the intentions and aims of the experiment. The Project qualified for state legal subsidy.

In 47 percent of the initial 208 cases, *both* parties wanted to negotiate. Ultimately, 66 cases led to agreement and a contract between parties.

The kind of agreements are as follows:

– Agreement concerning payment, 48 cases.

– Agreement concerning behavior, 11 cases.

– Agreement concerning payment and behavior, 2 cases.

– Agreement concerning work, 4 cases.

– Agreement by arbitration, 1 case.

Table 1 is a preliminary tabulation of offenses charged in the sample, and the extent of reaching agreement in each offense category. (The full evaluation report was published by the Research and Documentation Center of the Department of Justice in the fall of 1991).

Tentative Conclusions

During the experiment and afterwards some tentative conclusions were drawn.

1 In police magistrate cases victims and offenders seemed to have a marked preference for mutual arrangement/agreement. Availability of certain resources (e.g. free legal assistance) facilitate this choice.

2 When people had expressed a willingness to negotiate, almost two-thirds of the negotiations were successful.

3 The highest percentage of parties dropping out were at the phase of initial contact with the parties.

Table 1: Outcomes of Dading by Case

OFFENSES	CASES	AGREEMENTS	
		N	%
PROPERTY	**108**	**30**	**27.8**
Theft	20	5	25.0
Shoplifting	36	9	25.0
Theft out of car	13	2	15.4
Burglary	33	11	33.3
Embezzlement	4	2	50.0
Fencing	2	1	50.0
PERSON	**67**	**21**	**31.3**
Maltreatment	53	16	30.2
Attempted manslaughter/ Severe maltreatment	9	3	33.3
Menace	5	2	40.0
VANDALISM	**30**	**11**	**36.7**
REMAINING	**9**	**4**	**44.4**
TOTAL	**214˙**	**66**	**30.8**

*This table contains six double countings compared with the number, 208, mentioned before. This is due to the fact that, in some cases with more than one suspect, not all of them did come to an agreement with the victim. In those cases, both agreement and failure are included.

4 In most cases agreements were fulfilled without major problems.

5 As far as we can ascertain the voluntary nature of participation parties was demonstrable in most cases. There are some doubts in cases of:

 – Victims of offenses taking place within relationships; in those cases pressure on the victim by the suspect to cooperate could not be precluded.

 – Suspects of shoplifting; in those cases a more or less standardized offer was made by the corporation victimized. The suspect had little choice but to take or leave the offer.

6 Ratification of a *dading* (settlement) instead of penal prosecution depends on:

 – Timely information by the Public Prosecutor. This not only refers to the time that is involved with negotiating, but also with the lapse of time since the offense was charged.

 – Accessibility of information and advice on how negotiation can be achieved instead of prosecution.

 – Accessibility of affordable, creative legal assistance.

7 The danger remains that *dadings* may, in some cases, be licenses for the offender to continue harming the victim in an ongoing relationship – a question which bears further investigation by category of offense.

NOTES

1 A police magistrate is a judge in the Dutch penal system who administers 'minor' offenses (maximum penalty imposed is six months imprisonment).

6 The New Outlawry and Foucault's Panoptic Nightmare

Steve Russell

Both civil law and common law provided for a diminution of citizenship rights based upon misconduct. Under Roman law, in which the civil law is rooted, citizenship might be wholly lost or simply diminished (Mackeldey 1883: 135). In common law countries, a citizen might, because of misconduct, become completely estranged from the community, a status called 'outlawry.'

> Such *outlawry is putting a man outside the protection of the law, so that he is incapable* to bring any action for redress of injuries; and it is also attended with a forfeiture of all one's goods and chattels to the king (Blackstone 1768: 284).

Outlawry was a powerful punishment to those few citizens who had a stake in feudal society. To a person who owned nothing and had no access to law in the best of times, a more salient feature of the King's justice was its power to torture and to kill, a power commonly exercised before the rise of imprisonment as an alternative.

The power of life and death contained within it the power to imprison. And if 'the body of the condemned' (Foucault 1975/1979) could be dismembered, it could also be set to labor to benefit the sovereign (Melossi and Pavarini 1977/1981). Since the dungeon was an impractical way to house workers, the penitentiary, as an exercise in social policy has also become an exercise in architecture.

As the penitentiary caught on in the United States, '... prison architecture and arrangements became the central concern of reformers of the period' (Rothman 1971: 83). A great policy debate between backers of the

Auburn (New York) and Pennsylvania models for prison construction raged for many years in the United States, a debate that largely ignored an English design thought by its author to embody the final solution to most problems in prison architecture.

The Panopticon was Jeremy Bentham's architectural innovation, a central tower within a circle of pie-slice cells where a small number of guards could observe, 'inspect' a much larger number of prisoners. This is not just the exercise in efficiency, Michel Foucault perceived, but an intensification of the power relationship by '... dissociating the seen/being seen dyad: in the peripheric ring, one is totally seen, without ever seeing; in the central tower, one sees everything without ever being seen' (Foucault 1975/1979: 1). To see in this sense is to discipline; to watch is to order, to keep track of, to put in place, to keep in place. For Foucault, this panoptic discipline is a metaphor for much of what really controls behavior in any post-industrial society.

While he was proud of the Panopticon and eager to put it to work, Bentham saw only a prison or a workhouse for paupers.

> The building *circular* – the cells occupying the circumference – the keepers, etc. – the centre – an *intermediate annular well*, all the way up, crowned by a *sky-light* usually open, answering the purpose of a *ditch* in *fortification,* and of a *chimney* in *ventilation* – the cells, laid *open* to it by an iron *grating.*

> The *yards* without, laid upon the same principle: – as also the *communication* between the buildings and the yards.

> By *blinds* and other contrivances, the keeper concealed from the observation of the prisoners, unless where he thinks fit to show himself: hence, on their part, the sentiment of an invisible omnipresence ….(Bentham 1843: 206)

'The Panopticon,' said Foucault, 'is a marvelous machine which, whatever use one may wish to put it to, produces homogeneous effects of power' (1975/1979: 202). But Foucault's primary interest was in '[t]he minute disciplines, the panopticisms of every day …' (p. 223).

> Take, for example, the ubiquitous case file, wherein … the child, the patient, the madman, the prisoner, were to become, with increasing ease from the eighteenth century and according to a curve which is that of the mechanisms of discipline, the objects

of individual descriptions and biographical accounts. This turning of real lives into writing is no longer a procedure of heroization; it functions as a procedure of objectification and subjection. (Foucault 1975/1979: 192).

The subjection we are discussing here is not the subjection of the Soviet Gulag, paved with case files. And the advocates of excessive order in our society are not unaware of the place surveillance enjoys in their scheme (Churchill and Wall 1990). The case file is an indispensable instrument of discipline.

In my jurisdiction, a reported felony creates a file with the city police. If a suspect is arrested, a file is created with the Sheriff, who runs the jail, and the magistrate who accepts the accusation, as well as with the District Attorney. If an indictment is returned, the District Clerk creates a file and a conviction means the probation office must open a file to do a presentence investigation, and potentially, the department of corrections will create a file which eventually spawn a parole file. If children are involved, if official corruption is involved – any number of 'ifs' can result in another file in another agency documenting one incident in one citizen's life and intersecting with other files on other criminals, victims, investigations, crimes and incidents in ways that can be collated and cross-referenced to formulate governmental policies of control.

Each exertion of State power creates another datum, another bit of knowledge and, of necessity, a Kafkaesque breach between the known and the knower. Computers never forget unless so instructed, and seldom are they so instructed. This has led to my many surreal experiences of opening a file in the presence of a citizen and 'remembering' *more of his history than he remembers.*

This is happening in a liberal democracy, not in some totalitarian dystopia, and Foucault himself clearly shared the revulsion that has been, since Solzhenitsyn, packed into the word 'Gulag.' 'The Gulag,' said Foucault in a 1977 interview, 'is not a question to be posed for any and every country. It has to be posed for every *socialist* country, insofar as none of these since 1917 has managed to function without a more-or-less developed Gulag system' (1980: 137). To discuss panopticism must not be to point fingers at others, to use Marxism or fascism as, in Foucault's phrase,' ... a floating signifier, whose function is essentially that of denunciation' (ibid.: 139).

If Foucault had lived to see the Eastern Bloc crumble from within, he probably would not have seen it as an aleatory event. He saw those nations as being in the horse-and-buggy era in the matter of repression. Direct and excessive use of governmental force is not merely immoral – it is *inefficient*. It is "... more efficient and profitable in terms of the economy of power to place people under surveillance than to subject them to some exemplary penalty' (ibid.: 38).

Studs Terkel, interviewing a telephone operator, elicited this example of panopticism at its most efficient:

> This company is the kind who watches you all the time. The supervisor does listen to you a lot. She can push a button on this special console. Just to see if I'm pleasant enough, if I talk too much to the customers, if I'm charging the right amount, if I make a personal call.
>
> Ma Bell is listening. And you don't know. That's why it's smart to do the right thing most of the time. Keep your nose clean. (1972: 69)

Ma Bell's execution of the panoptic principle here exceeds Bentham's technological reach.

> In his first version of the *Panopticon*, Bentham had also imagined an acoustic surveillance, operated by means of pipes leading from cells to the central tower. In the *Postscript* he abandoned the idea, perhaps because he could not introduce into it the principle of dissymmetry and prevent the prisoners from hearing the inspector as well as the inspector hearing them. (Foucault 1975/ 1979:317, n.3)

This is dissymmetrical listening and dissymmetrical watching in an utterly random fashion. Power creates knowledge which creates power. Big Brother (Orwell 1949) is not the only one watching; *anyone* might be watching. Or they might not. So it is best to keep one's nose clean.

Kafka (1925/1937) understood panopticism. Joseph K., awaiting trial before an invisible court on unknowable charges, is always the object rather than the subject. His every attempt to take charge of the process, to become the doer rather than the done to (and done for) sinks him more deeply into irrationality. His lack of knowledge makes his lack of power a foregone conclusion. Something is happening, and everyone seems to know what it is except the person to whom it is happening.

Kafka's name is eponymous for that feeling of falling through some existential void, of feeling there is some pattern behind apparent absurdity but knowing that trying to discover it would be a futile enterprise. Futility in the face of the absurd is what the powerful find salutary for the powerless, and accepting absurdity as normal is the ultimate submission to authority.

We see nothing sinister in this arrangement as applied to prisons; there is not only efficiency but justice in forging chains in the minds of known criminals. 'There is no risk,' said Foucault, '... that the increase of power created by the panoptic machine may degenerate into tyranny; the disciplinary mechanism will be democratically controlled ...' (1975/ 1979: 207). And there is no question that, according to our shared system of values, convicted criminals have a greatly diminished expectation of privacy (*Hudson* v. *Palmer*, 468 U.S. 517, 1984; *Bell* v. *Wolfish*, 441 U.S. 520, 1979).

Most citizens would carry this a step further and agree that criminals at large in the community cannot reasonably expect privacy, at least privacy for their criminal activity. 'There is a major difference ... between 'Big Brother' watching *everything* and government being able to detect *only* evidence of crime' (Loewy 1983: 1246). This might be called the silver bullet theory of the Fourth Amendment: a method of search that can discover nothing but contraband – say, a *perfect* drug-sniffing dog (*United States* v. *Place*, 462 U.S. 696, 1983) – is always reasonable. It is also archetypal panoptic discipline, since the inspected must always anticipate the inspection and may never see the inspector. The silver bullet aspect, the aiming of the intrusion only at the guilty, makes the random inspection acceptable to the courts and to public opinion.

Random urine testing on the job is fair, assuming perfect chemical tests, because it affects no one but drug users. Pre-employment psychological screening is fair, assuming perfect diagnostic instruments, because it weeds out only persons no sensible employer would want to hire. No one need fear polygraph examination except liars. A telephone operator will never know her supervisor is listening unless she violates the rules.

The perfection of silver bullet technology logically leads to reversing the hoary principle that a search cannot be justified by what turns up (*Sibron* v. *New York*, 392 U.S. 40, 1968; *Byars* v. *United States*, 273 U.S. 28, 1927). If arguments against any particular form of surveillance are directed at flaws in the technology, the argument can quickly become one about how much less than perfection is acceptable. We do, after all, accept capital punishment, and very few workers within the criminal justice system believe that it finds facts perfectly – or that they could really trust *their own* lives to it.

It is for most of us not a question of what is being done, but to whom. Like Joseph K., we do not expect to ring for our breakfast and be confronted by the authorities. For criminals, such happenings are an occupational hazard. As we do not expect to be treated like criminals, they should not expect to be treated like us. Outlawry is not an outmoded concept in the area of privacy. A criminal is properly subject to surveillance by a probation officer (*Griffin* v. *Wisconsin*, 483 U.S. 868, 1987) as is a welfare client by her case worker (*Wyman* v. *James*, 400 U.S. 309, 1071) or a student by his teachers (J. Noble and W. Noble, 1980). An alien – the quintessential anonymous other – may lawfully be held incommunicado until s/he defecates into a waste basket, under surveillance! (*United States* v. *De Hernandez*, 473 U.S. 531, 1985).

Surveillance is the common element in most of our cutting-edge alternatives to incarceration – electronic monitoring being the most obviously intrusive. Surveillance, especially when used to deinstitutionalize mental patients, is functioning here in the service of humane impulses, just as prisons and mental hospitals originally did (Rothman 1971). Giving rein to these impulses may be the proper thing to do, but if so, we should do it with open eyes, realizing that we are creating a constitutional underclass, further obscuring lines of privacy that exist only imperfectly for persons who have been found guilty of no misconduct. Accepting panoptic discipline for anyone starts us down a slippery slope from criminal to mental patient to soldier to employee to student to ordinary citizen. 'Is it surprising,' Foucault asked, 'that prisons resemble factories, schools, barracks, hospitals, which all resemble prisons?' (1975/1979: 228).

One answer to slippery-slope reasoning might be called spikes-on-our-boots: the feared result will not happen if we stoutly resolve not to let it happen. Unfortunately, the United States Supreme Court in *Laird* v. *Tatum* (408 U.S. 1, 1972) has clipped the best spike from our boots by refusing to recognize in the constitution the right of privacy – the right of innocent citizens to be free of governmental surveillance.

More precisely, the Court created an insurmountable barrier for any citizen ever asserted such a right, if it exists. The plaintiffs – victims of surveillance by the US Army – argued that the mere existence of governmental surveillance had a chilling effect on their rights to freedom of association, speech, and the press, all guaranteed by the First Amendment. The Court found that the mere existence of the lawsuit rebutted the plaintiffs' claims of a chilling effect on their constitutional rights; since the plaintiffs were not harmed, they had no standing to sue.

In *Laird* v. *Tatum*, the Supreme Court has created one of the great jurisprudential Catch-22s of all time: chilled citizens will not sue and citizens who are not chilled have no standing to sue. By demanding a more tangible harm than chilling effect, the Court has legalized governmental surveillance by taking away the means for declaring it to be illegal. Justice William O. Douglas observed correctly in dissent that such a standing requirement '... would in practical effect immunize from judicial scrutiny all surveillance activities, regardless of their misuse and their deterrent effect' (408 U.S. at 26).

The possibilities of 'misuse' or even 'deterrent effect' are not really the point. These possibilities link the question of governmental surveillance to what an honest citizen would want to hide. Our need for privacy, if it must be justified to the government, has no sanctity as a fundamental principle and little chance of recognition by executives, legislatures, or courts. Foucault reminded us that the question of surveillance (knowledge) is a question of power, distribution or power between the government and the governed. Justice Douglas, dissenting in *Laird* v. *Tatum*, articulated one view of the appropriate distribution:

> This case involves a cancer in our body politic. It is a measure of the disease which afflicts us. Army surveillance, like Army regimentation, is at war with the principles of the First Amendment. Those who already walk submissively will say there is no cause for alarm. But submissiveness is not our heritage. The First Amendment was designed to allow rebellion to remain as our heritage. The Constitution was designed to keep the government off the backs of the people. The Bill of Rights was added to keep the precinct of belief and expression, of the press, of political and social activities free from surveillance. The Bill of Rights was designed to keep agents of government and official eavesdroppers away from assemblies of people. The aim was to allow men to be free and independent and to assert their rights against government. (408 U.S. at 28)

Other respectable views of the appropriate distribution of power between government and the people are common, which is why Justice Douglas expressed his in dissent. But the debate about surveillance is a debate about power, and one word for a society in which governmental surveillance may not be challenged in court is 'panoptic.' Bentham's efforts to gain governmental imprimatur for the Panopticon stirred up the issue of power, even in the heyday of the utilitarians.

> There was no question of the 'rights' of prisoners and paupers, for there was no such thing as rights at all. There were only interests, and the interests of the majority had to prevail. The greatest happiness of the greatest number might thus require the greatest misery of the few.

> The principle of the greatest happiness of the greatest number was as inimical to the idea of liberty as to the idea of rights. Just as Bentham attacked those parents whose scruples about liberty made them apprehensive of a panopticon-school, so he attacked those who expressed the same scruples and apprehensions in matters of government. (Himmelfarb 1968: 77)

With federal and state prison populations rising 115 percent between 1980 and 1990 (DeWitt 1990), it is fair to question how many scruples and apprehensions about surveillance we can afford. The cost of incarcerating even a fraction of the 2.7 million Americans on probation or parole would be staggering. Numbers of persons under court-ordered surveillance, therefore, rise as quickly as surveillance becomes available. Use of electronic monitoring – a technology only available since 1984 – climbed about 300 percent between 1988 and 1989 (Schmidt 1989).

Persons under court-ordered surveillance are, in terms of most rights to privacy, the new outlaws – their homes, financial affairs, sex habits, and bodily fluids subject to inspection by the government. We have outlawed, in this sense, shocking percentages of some subgroups – 33.2 percent of young black males in California, for example (Fry and Schiraldi 1990). This disparate impact on some communities may or may not be the result of differing patterns of criminality, but the sheer numbers of all people under surveillance-as-punishment combined with the Supreme Court's position in *Laird* v. *Tatum* that governmental surveillance is constitutionally benign are ample cause to apprehend panopticism as not just a design for a prison, but a design for a society.

Panoptic architecture might be dismissed as an overblown metaphor, but the digital computer – the simple ability to count great numbers of like occurrences – has given eyes to power beyond Bentham's wildest dreams. Geographical distribution of crime is plotted by computer and used to assign police controls. Neighborhoods with more reported deviancy get more surveillance and therefore more reported deviancy. Computers find stolen property by tracking pawnshop transactions, while incidentally inspecting thousands of innocent loans. In a country where the freedom of interstate travel is taken for granted, individual movements of most citizens who do travel are easily traced by credit card transactions. While the Panopticon made short-range and small-scale surveillance more efficient, computers and electronic communications could potentially make nationwide surveillance of whole communities and troublesome individuals nearly perfect.

This potential is far from realization because civil libertarians might have opposed it (Neier 1975) and because civil libertarians might dominate the political discourse if the government were to move into information technology on a grand and obviously intrusive scale. Foucault warned, however, that '... although the universal juridicism of modern society seems to fix limits on the exercise of power, its universally widespread panopticism enables it to operate, on the underside of the law, a machinery that is both immense and minute, which supports, reinforces, multiplies the asymmetry of power and undermines the limits that are traced around the law' (1975/1979: 223).

It is probably a good thing that power may assert itself in ways that are more economical and less barbaric, but the 'panopticisms of every day' are no less intrusive for their subtlety. We should be thankful for Foucault's forceful reminder that *surveiller* is to assert power. A decision about surveillance is a decision about apportionment of power, and once a citizen has to justify privacy, to say what might be hidden from the government, *power has already been apportioned*.

Surveillance is not omnipresent but not omniscient. Bentham failed to achieve perfect panoptic discipline for lack of technology; we fail only because of a lack of political will. Foucault does not condemn this state of affairs; he merely describes it, and only our political principles can determine whether Foucault's description is a nightmare or a dream or just an invitation to wake up.

REFERENCES

Bell v. *Wolfish*, 441 U.S. 520. 1979

Bentham, J. 1843. 'Panopticon Papers,' in M.P. Mack, ed., *A Bentham Reader*, 189-208. New York: Pegasus

Blackstone, W. 1768. *Commentaries on the laws of England*. Vol. 3. Facsimile ed. London: University of Chicago Press

Byars v. *United States*, 273 U.S. 28. 1927

Churchill, W., and J.V. Wall. 1990. *The COINTELPRO Papers: Documents From the FBI's Secret Wars Against Domestic Dissent*. Boston: South End Press

DeWitt, C.B. 1990. *National Institute of Justice Construction Bulletin*. Available from US Department of Justice, Office of Justice Programs, Washington, D.C. 20531

Foucault, M. 1979. *Discipline and Punish: The birth of the Prison*. A. Sheridan, trans. New York: Random House. (Original work published 1975)

– 1980. 'Powers and Strategies,' in C. Gordon (ed.) *Power/Knowledge: Selected Interviews and Other Writings*, 134-145. C. Gordon, trans. New York: Pantheon Books. (Original work published 1977)

Fry, S. and V. Schiraldi. 1990. *Young African American Men and the Criminal Justice System in California*. Available from National Center on Institutions and Alternatives, Western Regional Office, 1165 Harrison Street, San Francisco, California 94103

Griffin v. *Wisconsin*, 483 U.S. 868. 1987

Himmelfarb, G. 1968. 'The Haunted House of Jeremy Bentham,' in (AUTHOR,)*Victorian Minds*, 32-81. New York: Alfred A. Knopf

Hudson v. *Palmer*, 468 U.S. 517. 1984

Kafka, F. 1937. *The Trial*. W. Muir and E. Muir, trans. New York: Schocken Books. (Original work published 1925)

Laird v. *Tatum*, 408 U.S. 1. 1972

Loewy, A.H. 1983. 'The Fourth Amendment as a Device for Protecting the Innocent.' *Michigan Law Review, 81*: 1229-1284

Mackeldey, F. 1883. *Handbook of the Roman Law*, M. Dropsie, trans. Philadelphia: T. and J. Johnson. (Original work published 1814)

Melossi, D. and M. Pavarini. 1981. *The Prison and the Factory: Origins of the Penitentiary System*, G. Cousins, trans. London: The Macmillan Press. (Original work published 1977)

Neier, A. 1975. *Dossier: The Secret Files They Keep on You.* New York: Stein and Day

Noble, J. and W. Noble. 1980. 'Surveillance: Its Cost to Education." in J. Noble and W. Noble, eds., *The Private Me*, 173-182. New York: Delacorte Press

Orwell, G. 1949. *Nineteen Eighty-Four.* New York: Harcourt, Brace and World

Rothman, D.J. 1971. *The Discovery of the Asylum: Social Order and Disorder in the New Republic*, revised ed. Boston: Little, Brown

Schmidt, A.K. 1989. 'Electronic Monitoring of Offenders Increases.' *NIJ Reports*, 212: 2-5

Sibron v. *New York*, 392 U.S. 40. 1968

Solzhenitsyn, A. 1973. *The Gulag Archipelago 1918-1956: An Experiment in Literary Investigation*, T.P. Whitney, trans. New York: Harper and Row

Terkel, S. 1972. *Working.* New York: Avon Books

United States v. *De Hernandez*, 473 U.S. 531 (1985)

United States v. *Place*, 462 U.S. 696. 1983

Wyman v. *James*, 400 U.S. 309. 1971

7 A Postmodern Challenge or the Seducing Other: From the Politics of the Unfinished to the Politics of Undecidability

Ari Hirvonen

Prology and Epilogy

'My writing' will be about a movement in a double sense. First, it will outline or trace a movement from the modern critical legal/social theory/practice to post-modern 'legal' strategies, movement from description to irony, from political to trans-political, from 'moralism' to 'nihilism.' Secondly, it will do this through 'deconstructing' the movement of abolitionism and its way of reading the legal/social control (con)texts.

'My writing' is not about the history or even of the genealogy of critical/radical practices in the area of justice. It is 'a case study' (empirical + theoretical = speculative) of one narrative, a reading of a short story about the abolition of the (criminal) law.

Why the criminal law, why the movement of abolitionism, you may ask. I could argue that in the criminal law the repressive function and de-socializing effects of the modern, bureaucratic, and non-discursive law are openly in the stage; or that it legitimizes the use of violence by the state; or that, in last instance, it secures the function of law in general (this is a mirror image of materialism: the criminal law is the basic structure of the legal society, in which other parts of the legal system are based).

Or I could argue that abolitionism is the most radical social/legal theory and practice in the 'history' of critical jurisprudence (or could be if one would radicalize its movements by re-reading it).

But I will not do that (while doing it) because I do not know if these kind of legitimations of 'my writing' are necessary/effective/'true.' The decision is arbitrary.

This is not about the philosophy of law but it has something to do with the modern philosophical closures that one can read from abolitionism. If you want to read this writing more generally, if you want to find from it traces which have something to do with the general critical legal theory, you can do it (of course I am not present to give you permission). Maybe it is just a movement from some-where to no-where; a blind example that seduces only its writer: the so called 'I,' seduces this 'I' so much that it writes this again (and again).

'My writing' will be about flows. This movement is also a movement from the fixed identity of Norma Jean to forever moving identity of Marilyn. It will read out images of abolitionism, which one-does-not-know thoroughly: those who know me as heterogeneous strategies, know better how to abolish.

Marilyn Meets Jacques

Marilyn Monroe once said: 'Those who know me better, know better.' But who is the subject who knows better, who is the object to be known. Only frustration appears when the object flees the knowing subject: Marilyn as an object impossible to know seduces knowledge; only altering images and 'free-play' of styles appear when the Man-of-Science tries to tell us the truth about the object (or about the 'real person'). The Judaeo-Christian, or the bourgeois, or the Cartesian (whatever she wants) idea of the individual as a unity has been sent into crisis.

If Marilyn seduces us, then the Law produces us; the law which also produces crisis-criticism, deviancy, subversions and revolutions. Everything is 'culturally hypnotized' i.e., we have an inescapable tendency to see and experience reality as we are programmed to see and experience it (Daudi 1988: 2). The Other of the Law is no more 'emancipated' than the law. The law needs the Other, the Other the law and back again.

The laws of genre/gender, the laws of reading/looking (or if you want acting/emancipation) position bodies and writing in defined relations. These laws also write the Other, the fixed and stable Other, which is nothing more than the negative of the code and norm. There is nothing secret or]subversive' in this Other, this Other which is 'the real person behind the images': those who know me better, know better the law.

For the late French psychoanalyst, Jacques Lacan, human knowledge (*connaissance*) is inextricably bound up with '*meconnaissance*' (misconstruction, failure to recognize). This *meconnaissance* constitutes the ego and its objects with attributes of permanence, identity, and substantiality. The illusion of autonomy is behind knowledge of reality, things, and oneself (Lacan 1977: 107). And there – do you really know that? – Marilyn who seduces us: those who know me as a 'free-play' of signs, styles, and images, know better, or those who (as I do) do not know me (thoroughly), know better. Jacques knows Marilyn better because he does not know the true person, or he knows that the true person is a series of misconstructions and illusions of stability.

Marilyn's and Jacques' other differs from the Other of the Law. For Lacan the other is something one-does-not-know (which escapes attempts to reduce it, attempts of understanding, attempts of the law of identity and stability); it is the locus of the speech, the addresses of the demand; and according to Lacan, one's desire is the desire of the Other.

This other is a 'field' of different and heterogeneous forces and 'differences.' It is something that is not fixed and stable, something that has no identity, or which is not reducible by the language of science, sociology, and philosophy. The other is a flow of unreadable texts, indecisiveness, unconscious, etc. The discourse of the other, as of Marilyn, is a multiplicity of free wheeling styles, genres, genders, forms, perspectives, and positions. Discourse of the other is at the same time oppressed by the law, and it precedes the law, or the dichotomy of the (stable) Law/Other, and that is why it is outside the control of the Law and the dichotomy coded by the Law.

'My writing' will be about movements or flows. It will outline or trace a movement from the modern critical social theory/practice to a postmodern strategies, movement from description to irony, from politics to trans-politics, from 'moralism' to 'nihilism'. This movement is also a movement from the fixed identity of Norma Jean to the forever moving identity of Marilyn.

In 'particular' it will re-read or 'deconstruct' the texts and/or genre of abolitionism, or it will trace multiple paradigms and images of abolitionism, which one-does-not-know thoroughly: those who know me as heterogeneous strategies, know better how to abolish.

The Identity of Abolition

'Abolish' comes from Latin word *ab-olere*: 'to grow out of use.' The Oxford English Dictionary defines it as: 'to put an end to, to do away with, to annul or make void, to demolish, destroy, or annihilate ... it is usually said of institutions, customs, and practices.'

I will write about abolition in a double sense. First, I will write about abolition as a political/theoretical movement or as a critical legal and social theory. The word abolition was first used in this sense in connection with the movement which tried to abolish the slave trade at the end of 18th century. Nowadays, it is a movement which aims to abolish capital punishment, the prison system, the criminal law, etc.

Depending who is speaking it means:

1 *deinstitutionalizing*, i.e. abolishing prisons, asylums, mental hospitals etc.,

2 *decriminalization*, i.e. decriminalizing certain crimes,

3 *decategorizing*, i.e. to get rid of the categorizing language of the penal law and also other parts of the law (categorizing effects of the private law, the regulation concerning social security, etc.),

4 *deformalizing*, i.e. that the conflicts between people could be handled and solved informally without interference from legal institutions,

5 *demystifying*, i.e. to destroy and deconstruct the ideology of the law to delegitimize its objectivity,

6 *destructuring*, i.e. destructure the ways and discourses through which criminality, crime, and criminal are produced as social and cultural phenomena, and

7 *delegalizing*, i.e. abolition of the law and the legal way of thinking in various degrees: from a literal abolition of the criminal law to an anarchistic abolition of the modern justice system.

Secondly, I will write about abolition not as an 'active' movement, but as a 'passive' process in which I shall activate the 'meaning': 'to grow out of use.' I shall ask the modernist project and its ideas about the evolution, reason, and logic grown out of use in post-modern theory/reality.

L'Écart Absolu: Feminism

Abolition is – of course, you say to me – only 'one' subversive strategy among others, which aims at 'liberating,' freeing the Other. The Other about which it writes is deviancy, criminality, insanity, and madness.

The Other which, in society, is put behind the walls of prisons, mental hospitals; the other which, in scientific discourse, is put under the name of fiction; the other, which in interpersonal relationships, is put under the label of irrelevancy and intrapersonally, this other is closed in the subconscious behind the walls of a culturally hypnotized fixed individual.

Other subversive strategies speak for/from/about different others: the other can be assigned to woman, to femininity, to children, to youth, to unconsciousness, to passion, to body, to *chor*, etc. The Other and the emancipation, the strategy of subversion and being beyond domination: impossible (is it?) but ah, so seducing .... But subversive strategies 'must' also move from the concept of the fixed other (the deviant/the feminine/ the unconscious) to the idea about otherness as a flow, and as strategy as a heterogeneous and multiple movement. The strategy of the other also needs other strategies. Here I will compare other as the feminine to the other of abolitionism. What I write to you – you as 'my' other – is about the structuring and differences of abolition and about the 'sameness' of structuring of different subversive genres of otherness.

Feminism can be divided into three phases according to French psychoanalyst Julia Kristeva (1986). The first phase of feminism is committed to the struggle for equality for women. It demands equal political, social, and economic rights and at the same time it is an effort to make women become like men. The contemporary symbolic order is taken as a norm; male standards and values are something to be achieved.

The second phase is a reaction against equality-feminism: it emphasizes the value of women as they are, on their own terms. This value is located in difference, not in equality as in first phase. The male as a law and norm is left behind. Different (i.e. feminine) ways of reading, writing, doing politics, etc. are preferred.

The third phase of feminism is deconstruction. It deconstructs all identities, phallocentric logic, and binary oppositions (like man/woman, soul/body, reason/passion). It is interested in how sexual identity is produced (through lack, through symbolic order, through language, etc.) and tries to locate the place of the subject's division.

The 'concept' feminine (or woman) differs radically from feminism's traditional, stable, and consistent concept. This new idea/concept is made possible by coding the radical otherness as feminine. This deconstructed feminine avoids the logocentric and phallocentric logic of the contemporary symbolic order (or makes its absolute reign open to doubt and disturbs it). The metaphor for the feminine is dance (dis-tanz = at the same time, dance and distance in the male society), which avoids conceptualizations and the logic of binary oppositions; when in the second phase the opposition was inverted and the 'inferior' term (woman) was established on top, now the question of what opposition is asked: it begins to shift the conceptual ground wherein its foundations are laid. Instead of becoming it is de-coming.

Scholars in the USA and France take special interest in reading and re-writing (*ecriture feminine*) psychoanalytical texts, and especially texts by Lacan. Jane Gallop (1985: 20) writes:

> My assumption of my inadequacy (that everyone, regardless of his or her organs, is 'castrated') and my attempt to read from that position are thus, to my mind, both Lacanian and feminist.

In the third space, there is 'a parallel existence of all three in the same historical time, or they may even be interwoven one with the other' (Kristeva 1986: 209). And this can mean that, in the third phase, there is the parallel existence of feminism, deconstruction, and Lacanian psychoanalysis.

In feminist legal theory, one can find a similar structure. According to American legal theorist, Frances Olsen, first phase is legal reformism. She writes:

> The first category consists of those critiques that attack the claim that law is rational, objective, abstract and principled, while agreeing that rational, objective, etc. is better than irrational, subjective, etc. These feminists argue that law should be rational, objective, principled and struggle to improve the lot of women by trying to make law live up to its claims and actually be rational, objective, and principled. (1990: 205)

The second phase sees law as patriarchy. They:

> accept that law is rational, objective, and principled but reject the hierarchization of the dualisms, feminists holding this view characterize law as male and patriarchal, and thus ideologically oppressive to women. (ibid.)

The third strategy is critical legal theory, which:

rejects the hierarchy of rational, objective, etc. over irrational, subjective, etc. and denies that law is or could be rational, objective, abstract and principled .... They disagree, however, that law is male; law has no essence or immutable nature. Law is a form of human activity, a practice carried on by people – predominantly men. (ibid.: 208)

And this position is taken also by another American legal scholar Clare Dalton (1988: 285):

Law, like every other cultural institution, is a place where we tell one another stories about our relationships with ourselves, one another, and authority. In this, law is no different from the *Boston Globe*, the CBS evening news, *Mother Jones*, or a law school faculty meeting. When we tell one another stories, we use languages and themes that different pieces of culture make available to us, and that limit the stories we can tell. Since our stories influence how we imagine, as well as how we describe, our relationships, our stories also limit who we can be.

In abolition, I 'find' the same kind of structuring. The first phase of abolition is that of moralism. It has very concrete goals and is action-oriented. It is committed to the struggle for human equality, for free and just discourse in society. Its style or genre is poetry and its Utopia is poetic justice without written laws.

The second generation of abolition is that of ideologism. It is more theoretically or analytically oriented. Instead of equality, it is more interested in differences: human equality is not the ultimate signified; it tries to break away from unifying concepts and institutions to the appreciation of differences in the political society. Its style is politics and its Utopia is a just society/'socialism' with a large tolerance for 'deviants' or differences. We will defer the coming of the third position or the third phase (face) of abolition, and have a chat with the 'first' two faces.

The First Phase: Moralism

The first narrative of the modern abolition movement is interested in the relationship between morality and the law. It is based on a belief in the natural law which in turn is based on universal moral values and norms. According to this position, legal norms must be diverted from basic moral principles, and the legitimacy of the modern law depends on how it reflects these principles. If (and when) the (criminal, penal) law has no moral content (or it is somehow based on natural law) and if (and when) it is a pure exercise in political power and pain production, it should be abolished.

Instead of the natural law, one can also base one's arguments on the social contract, or to the pre-modern social order and discursive ethics. If the criminal law is not the result of open and free discourse about legal norms in society, it should be abolished.

In this narrative, a search is made for alternative means of solving conflicts, and through them, ways to abolish 'the pain' are established. In practice, abolition has to realize a non-repressive and non-punitive grammar. It should develop and, in its political and social activities, realize different 'counter-strategies' aimed at minimizing the area of criminal law and the repression and punitive system based on compulsion.

The social activities of abolition can be justified on the strangest of grounds: religious views are based on the grace of the *New Testament*; liberal moralists weep at the 'pain' caused by punishment; the 'habermasian' alternativists look for pure and human communication; and the anarchists, ensnared by their conviction, are against all that concerns the State. The choice is free, the aim is the same.

In this phase I examine the texts of Louk Hulsman (1982) and Nils Christie (1981). The abolition of penal law (and also the language and logic of the penal justice) is for Hulsman a logical necessity. The criminal law is still based on inquisition and its absolute language is repressive: it confuses reality with its classifications and definitions. Without this reductionist way of thinking, we are not able to understand better the surrounding reality, and then realize that the criminal law is only one way of reacting to social problems and contradictions.

If the criminal law were replaced by decentralized, autonomous, conflict-solving methods, the guilt principle would be replaced by a risk principle: problematic situations would be seen as catastrophes which everyone would hope would be solved. Thus many other socio-political problems produced by criminal law would also be abolished: marginalizing specific groups, producing and labeling offenders, producing ungrounded suffering divided unevenly between different social groups, etc. The penal law is unnecessary, it does not have a functional component which legitimizes and maintains the prevailing system, and thus its abolition would not produce any functional gap in the existing system's activities.

Christie's moralizing argumentation takes a negative standpoint on the punishment system which he claims has only destructive effects. Punishment means pain which should be minimized by looking for alternative ways for solving conflicts or by excluding the whole reaction. The penal law system steals conflicts from those directly concerned and, instead of solving conflicts, it only looks for an offender. Dialogy is offered as an alternative which enables the understanding of conflicts and produces solidarity between the parties involved. This corresponds very widely with Hulsman's understanding of collective discussion and of logic, free from the stereotypes of the criminal law.

Unofficial social control demands power and knowledge splitting nearer to a human being, to autonomous unities acting on the basis of near control. Christie reads in the same ethnocentric viewpoint as Hulsman: 'green' argumentations seek their justification in pre-industrial life styles and pre-modern society's social control. This idealization is then transferred in itself as a model and as a norm for contemporary post-modern culture.

The Second Phase: Ideologism

In the second phase of abolition, the relationship between a political/economic power and the law is the central issue. Legal norms are seen to be for securing certain material goals and a certain politico-economic structure.

The law (in various degrees) is regarded as a repressive and unfair machinery that, under the myth of objectivity, only strengthens the contemporary political order. In this narrative, the law and justice are in antinomical contradiction: by changing the legal system, legal norms, or legal principles, it is not possible to change the basic (and repressive) structure of an unjust society. Only minor changes are possible. That is why abolition of the law (in various degrees) is a political strategy which not only reduces the 'pain' that is created by legal institutions, but which also by abolishing the (repressive) law opens up the road to a more just society, to a more fair economic order.

This narrative analyzes historically 'repressive' structures and practices (language, justice, the criminal law, the penal system, the social security system, etc.), the genealogy of the institutions based on compulsion (prisons, mental hospitals, armies, schools, etc.) as well as discourse models that legitimate them. Moreover, it examines the texts ('reality') of existing power, control, and discipline without restricting itself only to the 'easy' and 'visible' areas of criminal law and prisons/penal system. But that is not enough ....

Many texts quoted in this narrative see the law as a monolithic, solid, and stable system with only repressive functions. A rigid analysis of the function and structuring of law and its heterogeneity (in the post-industrialized welfare state) would open up new paths for these political practices or for a social theory of abolition.

In this narrative, one can have different positions or approaches (the basic ideology which legitimates/justifies abolition): Marxism, feminism, structuralism, existentialism, 'genealogism,' etc. The way to read the 'control reality' or the 'language of control' is dependent upon these background truths of 'abolition.'

I now examine the texts of Michel Foucault (1977, 1977b) and Thomas Mathiesen (1974). In Foucault's theoretical and practical activities, we can find traces of abolition, even if he himself does not name it. He took part, for example, in the GIP (*Groupe d'Information sur les Prisons*), the aim of which was to produce counter-information concerning the official criminal policy and the conditions in French prisons. On the other hand it tried to create for prisoners, ex-prisoners, and their relatives the right and possibility to present their points of view. He also participated in various protests against prisons and repeatedly protested against the death penalty.

The abolition of the criminal law system or prisons is only a marginal part of abolition. It is important though, because, in prisons, power appears in its most naked state, in its most extreme form. Here power is justified as a moral principle. Instead of simplifying idealization, power should be examined at the micro level: one should study the manifold nets of social control extending to all areas of social life. By abolishing power which comes downwards like the criminal law system, we hold to the juridic-political definition of power and forget its disciplinatory role, its activity in producing knowledge and being produced by knowledge. For Foucault 'Abolition' thus acts in different power nets, it is a part of knowledge production and the exercise of power.

For Mathiesen, the abolition of prison is only a short term aim bound to widen in scope to the entire official control system, to the politics of compulsion, and to society's basic economic structures. Changing the prevailing system is an endless process, a project of continuous abolition. To remain unfinished it has to renew itself every moment. It has continuously to abolish more and more prevailing repressive structures and restrictions. Abolition opens up possibilities for the abolition of wider structures, and makes it, on the other hand, necessary, because attempts are always made to replace abolished structures with new conserving systems. Abolition has to oppose the values, interests, and basic structure of the contemporary system. It has to avoid not being defined in the system, in which case it will become a movement representing only reform politics. On the other hand, it has to be on its guard not to get defined out of the system, in which case its criticism will become irrelevant. The competing contradiction is Mathiesen's answer.

Mathiesen defines by means of materialistic 'slang' the law to be a phenomenon of economic structures which, in the end, are based on the ways of production. The changes in basic structures achieve changes in juridic structures, but the basic structures of society cannot, however, be changed by means of legislation.

The Post-Modern Break in Social Theory

We have to defer – always deferring – the coming of the third phase of abolition, and before that, read what postmodern 'means' before we can speak about a postmodern 'version' of abolition. Traditionally modern science has letigimated itself with the help of a meta-criterion of knowledge, i.e. a criterion of legitimate knowledge. Scientific discourses have legitimated themselves

> with reference to a meta-discourse ... making an explicit appeal to some grand narrative, such as the dialectics of the Spirit, the hermeneutics of meaning, the emancipation of the rational working subject, or the creation of wealth. (Lyotard 1984: xxiii).

From these 'post offices,' the clerks of philosophy have preached their Truths, and at the same moment justified their discourse. This never ending process of the production of knowledge is a mirror image of the logic of capitalism. The chain of investments and reinvestment of values, signs, and truths must never stop: To stop would be a catastrophe to modern philosophy. Produce more and more Truths, because without production there is no Reality-of-Truths. So please, buy me a brand new Cadillac ....

In legal theory, self-legitimation has happened either from inside the closed legal system by Grandmas of closed consensus, or by the Little Red Riding Hoods who have smuggled into legal theory the political, ideology, and moral values and principles. Abolition (if it has anything to do with legal theory) belongs to the latter genre.

Now we come to the 'third' phase, the challenge from the post-modern. Post-modernity has created a crisis in the legitimacy of all intellectual activities: the quest for truth has lost its value and the basis of all human knowledge is in a state of crisis. The major theories which legitimated the production of modern philosophy have disseminated, pulverized, and vanished.

The post-modern claim about the end of history or the end of great narratives signifies the dissolution of evolution as a unitary process. One can only refer back to the fragmented and differing narratives: everything is dissolved into discourses. There is no more final appeal to external referents or transcendental signifieds, no more can one speak about the true essence of hu-Man Beings.

Italian philosopher, Gianni Vattimo (1987), does not see this change as a negative one. According to Vattimo, the collecting and transmitting of information and its diffusion over the entire globe has multiplied the number of historical centers. Because of advances in communication, self-consciousness among people has increased and this has de-legitimized the modern, the modern large narratives of their legitimizing function which can no longer be sustained. People, according to Vattimo, see that we live in a society which is not based on objective nature or reason, but on convention. This dissolution means also that there is no modern search for truth: each claim of truth is internal to a certain discourse and is dependent for its dominance over alternatives.

French philosopher, Jean-Francois Lyotard (1984), also writes about the post-modernity that undermines the stable foundations of human knowledge in which the modern's project is/will be fragmented. The death of the Great Narratives of emancipation, etc. has opened a world of possibilities, from this death has been born an heterogeneity of language plays. Lyotard's post-modern is also a critical movement: it opposes all kinds of totalitarian systems and is against the reduction and restriction of language plays.

According to Lyotard, the (Habermasian) consensus in ethics of discourse and formal pragmatics leads to a bankruptcy of pluralism. The practical consensus is not in itself a 'wrong,' but as a formal principle it sets restrictions, which are both material and virtual. The consensus may be of use in some discourses, but not as a totalizing principle in every discourse, in the nature of every linguistic act. In his book, *Le Differend*, Lyotard tries to 'build' a theory about justness which is not bound to consensus.

Jacques Derrida writes about textuality, saying there is nothing outside the texts. But we must remember that his idea about the text is different from the traditional views. According to Derrida, the text is not marks on a piece of paper, a book, or an essay; it has no limits at all. The field of the text is always a field of forces: heterogeneous, differential, contradictory, open, etc. Capitalism, legal norms, legal theory, legal institutions, etc. are all part of the general text. Derrida's idea about textuality is quite 'near' Vattimo's and Lyotard's analysis of post-modern knowledge. Behind these 'positions' one can read an opening to anti-totalitarian, anti-consensus, anti-utopian discourses, and fairness/justness. From this we can proceed to a post-jurisprudential reading-strategy.

Writing always leads to a book in modern jurisprudence or in legal philosophy. It takes its position, posts up its formal rationalities, and stagnates at the same moment as it loses a movement appropriate to its texts. In the General P.O. the Father is working.

Another way of approaching the texts of legal theory and the production factories of truths is possible by means of 'sciences' of the texts. You can call, if you wish, this post-'position' or movement a post-modern textual theory, or a deconstruction.

Science and literature can not be told one from another anymore. Jurisprudential texts, like the texts of literature, are linguistic constructs and under the figurative play of language, i.e. subordinated to the metaphorical and metonymical structures of language. Scientific truths, or the history of humankind, are as 'true' as the texts of literature/narratives/myths. When the hidden forms and figures of scientific and logical languages are exposed, the texts of science turn out to be an 'endless reflection on its own destruction at the hands of literature' (De Man 1979: 115).

The traditional division in substance (emphasized by science) and expression (breach of literature) loses its meaning in this approach (or they are no longer separated). The engineers of science, who are still groping after the truth legitimated by rationality or by emancipation, remain under the laws of texts (but the author who does not hear the text is the one who speaks). The 'subconscious' elements of texts breaks the intentions of the author and the 'closed' definitions. Truthfulness is only a value each reader gives to the text when translating the writing into a Meaning. Behind this kind of 'truthfulness' and closure, there is no referent, behind this play of reading and re-writing, there is no reality. That is why the truth serum has no effects any more.

Derrida writes about iteration: texts can be repeated endlessly and always differently. The reiteration of a text, regardless of the writer, the reader, or context, means that the text can be repeated without its reference, without the matter to which it refers, without the original meaning and contents of the writer (Derrida 1977: 179). The texts cannot thus be comprehended as the communication of a thought or idea, not as the representation of pure sense. On the contrary, every reading produces new and again new significations. You, my reader, are writing these signs, giving truth values to them which 'my' text tries desperately to avoid.

The post-jurisprudence differs 'radically' from the positivistic-emancipatory narratives. Instead of the critical reading of the texts of the laws, 'analyzing' and 'deconstructing' the laws of the texts, the 're-writings' and the blind spots of the 'intentions/authors' are emphasized.

'Misreading' is reading in another way, it starts from the text itself, but not following the open stated intentions, its pretended closures, its 'constant meaning.' With a playful gaze and rigorous reading, points are looked for where the text breaks the rules it has defined for itself; breaks are looked for, which reveal the powers which have produced the text; a search is made for what is hidden and influences the structure, form, and 'contents' of the whole text. How the exhibition takes place and the nature of the centers directing the events of the scene – is the point of misreading. It can also be called a deconstruction of the text, its splitting up, the examination of its structure, binary opposition, and centers. It writes what is not said (in the text). All these conflicts and breaks already exist in the text itself, that is why it would be more 'right' to write about how the text deconstructs itself, and now, about how the interpreter deconstructs the text.

Using Heideggerian terms, one could speak about *An-denken* (re-thinking) and *Verwindung* (getting over) in this (con)text. Through re-thinking the histories of the law and problems of legitimacy of the law, through re-thinking the critical strategies (i.e. abolition); through re-thinking of the moral/natural or political/social challenges to the positive law, one can overcome the closures of the modern idea of the law.

A profound revision and transformation of the very notion of the law/justice begins by reading the confusion of meanings; multiplicity of discourses; and the conflicting visions of the law, legitimacy, and moral values. Speaking about the morality/legitimacy/rationality of the law is still believing in a reality from which legal discourse derives its representations: the law is then more or less a better representation of the social, economic, moral, or natural order, and it can also have some effects of these orders.

But if I reverse this picture (using Daguerre's camera), I can re-think the law as a simulation machine of the real, a part of the 'hyper-reality.' It is no longer a representation of the Real or the Truth, but a discourse that 'writes' the images of the social order. One can choose in which 'reality' one lives depending on what 'post office' one occupies. Daudi (1988: 3) writes:

> What we are left with is the possibility to accept or to reject any explanation, given the fact that whatever choice we make it will always be an arbitrary one without any more legitimate claim of truth than any other explanation.

Here we find the implosion of the law and begin the era of fragmented and different narratives of laws and moralities, but I will not go further in building a method of deconstruction. With my pogo stick, I shall jump from post-modern reading strategies to a de-constructive reading of abolition.

The Centers of the Modern Narrative of Abolition

Abolition includes contradictory, competing, and incompatible elements at the level of both theory and politic-moral 'truths' from which the aims are derived. In this sense, it is structured like the general legal theory and legal norms and principles. I will next read from the texts of abolition binary oppositions and the centers/the transcendental signifieds which close the free play or movement of these texts. By radicalizing the themes, and by reading what-is-written-to-texts-without-the-author's-intentions, or by analyzing the subconscious of texts, one can 'proceed' towards a trans-political social theory and visionary reading of the functions and effects of the law in contemporary mediocratia.

Concentrism. Instead of bourgeois-democratic consensus aimed at harmony, conflicts and problems are respected in abolition. Fragmented passions, unconscious desires, different interests, and competing individual morals are restored to social relations. (But beyond human consensus there is also the land of darkness and violence which abolition also opens to us).

Continuous (inter-and intra-) human coincidences are not only considered as negative phenomena, for suppressing of which social control equipment and education-machines are needed. Differences are natural as 'air and water': in them there is knowledge and through them solidarity can grow. Here abolition differs from 'traditional' critical theories aimed at changing social or physical structures to eliminate conflicts.

Abolition is therefore a challenge to unifying codes and political practices: beyond abolition of the penal law it also means the death of the Moral Code and Unified Reality. Texts speak about differences, about different ways of interpreting and understanding 'reality.'

'Anarchistic' voices aim disbelief towards the State. The State is considered as a monolithic administration factory which has stolen speech from the people. The constitutional state's written laws and institutionalized exercise of power offends and distorts authority, genuine sociality, and solidarity. By returning problem solving to the natural level, to the level of communication (i.e. spoken speech) free from economic-administrative interference, we can achieve genuine freedom, genuine sociality.

Hulsman however writes about replacing the criminal law by civil law. This illustrates the idea that the civil law is on the one hand based on the Social Contract, and on the other hand, it shows a belief in civil law's 'eunomistic' nature: the law should by its nature be reflexive, repairing, integrating, communicating, and stimulating. The criminal law, on the contrary, can be called, according to Durkheim's term, 'anomymal' law, that is, alienating and disintegrating law.

The Rousseauan division into 'present' speech (the civil law) and 'absent' writing (the penal law) can be seen very clearly in Hulsman's work (in the general from abolition). One should not take for granted this division and the illusion of the 'present' speech as being somehow better (or more natural) than the 'absent' writing. One should instead ask if the civil law really is a form of the 'present' speech or if this kind of (pseudo) difference or dichotomy has any meaning: what does it legitimate other than the contemporary logic of power and domination. But now, when I as a writer am absent, you as a reader – you who are present – must make your chase and destroy this illusion of 'natural' law/speech which could be somehow outside the power and oppression (of writing).

Producentrism. The final and binding social and political aims are missing from the texts. The instructions and alternative models are rather immediately situational than for building up absolute future views. Abolition continues the tradition of negative criticism (or even nihilism): it abolishes, destroys, deconstructs, and only after that, does it try to find where it is. There is no exact program for it. Even after that, it does not stop, because it must be an unfinished movement. Thus it challenges the closure of target-directed logic and rationality. But ....

The texts from which one can read narratives of abolitionism are written with strong connections to tales of emancipation, enlightenment, and change. The belief in the free Man, in knowledge free from ideology, in life free from power, in pure and free communication and solidarity are the topics which are revealed as motors of the text-machines. In the center, there is always the self-knowing I, logos, phallos, and sincere anthropocentric hu-MAN-ism. My gaze goes closer and looks at where this Grand Theory of the Modern speaks.

The modern belief in endless progression is engraved into the genetic code of abolition strategies and texts. The very work 'abolition' gives references: there are borders and the abolition of them is possible and even necessary for the critical and rational logos. Exceeding borders (prisons, penal law, etc.) give people more freedom, more authenticity, more rational communication instead of repressive language. Mathiesen and Foucault write about continuously abolishing the borders, about their continuous influence in one form or another. But in every case excess always produces 'positive' freedom.

These borders are repulsive to the abolitionist way of thinking and they are at the same time a stimulus making the slobber of criticism run and the abolitionist starts her 'affair': breaking the hymens of securities. In fact, abolition, especially as advertised by Thomas Mathiesen as an 'unfinished movement,' is a mirror image of the modern economic code of capitalism: economic growth is a necessary and positive phenomenon, with it the problems it causes can be solved. In other words the abolitionist suffers from a very modern disease: there is a feeling of angst if one is not free to add to production (of criticism, signs of progress, self understanding, etc.). Mathiesen is defined in the logic of Production, in the system that needs new (critical) signs all the time.

Logocentrism. When breaking the logic of criminalizing language, breaking up punishing institutes, and destroying police/constitutional states legislation's legitimation, abolition is now, however, driven into a crisis with its own strategy. It persistently believes in its superb virility to see and to talk beyond the logic of control in a reality determined by control's logic; it believes that its language is in a special way so sublime that by using it, we can transform and transcend the ideologically colored language of power. Abolitionists continually perform astonishing pirouettes when breaking the figures of the compulsory program. Unfortunately, it is not realized that every movement is based on the same language as the compulsory movements.

Abolition has the 'master' code by means of which the controlled texts and social reality can be rightly interpreted. The right interpretation correspondingly gives instructions for Rightful and Morally good innovations, in other words, in this connection, for the abolition of criminal law system.

There is an inner contradiction in abolition between the belief in truth-finding-project (or 'free speech'), and appreciation of conflicts. On the one hand, it writes about striking together (*com + fligere*) at the level of social relations, and on the other (same) hand, of thinking together (*com + sentire*) at the level of interpretation. Abolition is aimed at abolishing the ruling center (the penal law and its logic) determining the 'solving' conflicts, and thus 'freeing' differences. With another (same) movement, it demands for itself the right to interpret reality in a consensus producing way, and thus it excludes conflicts in the fields of interpretation, philosophy, and alternative politics. Abolition should move all the time from *sentire* to *fligere* and so stay unfinished. When it stops to secure consensus and belief in its language's freedom, it is defined a second time. The first time it is defined by language, the second time because it lives in an illusion of not being defined in, it re-produces consensus without noticing it itself.

The concept of respecting conflicts is contradictory with abolition's truthfulness. Abolition, on the one hand, talks of colliding with each other (*com + fligere*) at the level of social relations and on the other hand of thinking together (*com + sentire*) at the level of interpretation. Abolitionism is aimed at abolishing the ruling center determining and 'solving' conflicts thus trying to restore the mutual value of the conflicts due to them. With another movement, it demands itself the right to interpret reality in a consensus producing way thus excluding the respect of conflicts in the field of interpretation, philosophy and alternative politics.

Phonocentrism and Praxicentrism. The analysis of abolition would indicate that it is concentrated and bound with the pragmatic-political movement. Its aims have also influenced the formation of the theory and the stressing of historical analysis. It has as its background assumption, a belief in change and the idea that the structures and ways of thinking about societies can be changed by means of political activities. It has taken for granted that language is something which is under the control of the subject, not anything that precedes a subjects' being or which writes/creates the subject. The idea that a subject knows herself and her context is behind the modern story of abolition. Freudian psychoanalysis would teach something different to our self-knowing and fully modern male. But you – my dear reader – can read in the direction of *der Goldener Sigi*.

A kind of closure is demanded by abolition: division in text and practice; division in language and activity; division in analysis and participation is insuperable. One always governs the other one, and in abolition, it is the latter term, the latter function. A reluctance to accept theory (that is the subconscious fear of one's own inability to change one's own structuring, fear that one does-not-know oneself thoroughly) has influence, especially in political movements. Theory should stay in universities and libraries, says the abolitionist activist who continues: real activities take place in the streets, in every-day reality. While they are trying to kick the walls of prisons down, at the same time they are building walls between different activities.

Abolition of this closure is very hard because of subconscious fears, and it should be worked out in textual psychoanalysis of theory/practice. One should write again the contradiction between text and practice and see practice as a part of a general text because, in practice, you have to use concepts, ideas, significations, and other 'textual' elements. There is no practice outside the text. I shall leave this question open, but before going further we will have a few words with Derrida:

So, you share the impatience of those who would like texts to remain in the libraries, who would like text to signify 'book'. And you want this order maintained: let all those who concern themselves with texts understood in this latter sense [the 'deconstructionists'!] remain in their compartments, better yet in their departments! Let no 'deconstructionists' concern themselves with politics since, as we all know, don't we, deconstruction, difference, writing, and all that are [in the best of cases] politically neutral, ahistorical. (Derrida 1986; 169).

[Deconstructive readings] are not simply analyses of discourse .... They are also effective or active (as one says) interventions, in particular political and institutional interventions that transform contests without limiting themselves to theoretical or constative utterances even though they must also produce such utterances. (ibid.: 168).

And then Derrida (ibid.: 168) continues:

That's why I do not go 'beyond the text' in this new sense of the word text, by fighting and calling for a fight against apartheid, for example, I say 'for example' because it also happens that I become involved with institutional and academic politics or get myself imprisoned in Czechoslovakia for giving seminars prohibited by the authorities.

Penocentrism. The 'evil' (negative repression) is without exception the quality of juridic-political use of power. On the list of abolition we can put first the 'enemies of people' such as prisons, the criminal law as a punishing system, criminalization etc. The binary opposition between the law and social norms, the State and society, culture and nature, etc. are reproduced in this closure of abolition. The breaks for this can partly be found in Mathiesen's texts, in which he writes about abolition as an endless movement: after the abolition of prison new control forms are built which will come instead of it, which also have to be abolished, and especially from Foucault who writes about disciplinatory power affecting every sector and which is dissolved in the social body.

A Challenge to the Concept of Modern
Law and the Repression Hypothesis

If you still believe in a world where production and economy are central, where legislation works as a social steer, as a motor and overhead for anything, justice still has its position. French social theorist Jean Baudrillard (1983a) does not 'believe' in this. Justice is a 'factory' and prisons, the green-fields and money streams of the past. On the level of what used to be the non-essential sectors of capital, the global process of capital is founded. Media, fashion, publicity, information and communications networks and other reproductive 'factories' have compensated for production (also the production of legislation) as central elements of social growth of the image production. Models, forms, and codes compensate for the use and exchange value of the goods. The law should be included in these goods that have to be compensated for: the laws of signs replace the signs of the law. Nothing now flows according to its end or its social finality, they now all come from models.

'We' live in a world constructed out of models and simulations which have no referent or reality. Reality is produced and reproduced an indefinite number of times from information and memory factories, from models and miniaturized units. The simulation absorbs reality within itself: it is not a fiction or lie because in it, the difference between the real and the imaginary is imploded (ibid.: 11-13). This is 'hyper-reality,' 'the product of an irradiating synthesis of complimentary models in a hyper-space without atmosphere' (ibid.: 3).

Instead of the law people are homogenized in society according to the functional definition of their needs. Instead of economic, political and legislative power, reality is produced by the media, signs, and dominating cultural codes in the simulacrum. The law (with ends and social finalities) as a controlling instrument remains marginal in society. When all kinds of deviation have been coded and socialized in a common commune or in the *mediaiety*, the repressive control becomes a useless museum object. When the economic-cultural codes bind individuals in their positions, in the 'laws' of the codes of social 'development,' legislation as reformer of society receives only the token value of amusement.

If the prison was the model for the industrialized world and the law was the steering wheel of capital (or inversely), then the nuclear power plant is the model for the post-industrialized 'society': instead of the law, functional norms, security orders, codes, and architectural planning are the signifying mechanisms that 'write' the 'social' (con)text.

Or maybe the model is not even the nuclear power plant. Maybe the central point is the nucleus of the human cell. When there is no more critical distance (as in the world of laws) the model for 'society' is DNA, the master chemical that controls the development and functioning of organisms. Every difference is pre-coded, and deviancy is only a statistical category without any real effects. In the 'nucleus-society' normalized and (de-)socialized 'humans' are acting according to the rules of the codes and their only real referents are statistical roles and categories.

The marginal areas of power (and writing obituaries for the law) still remain the area for jurisprudence and legal philosophy. This idea also means that the critical legal strategies are fighting in areas which no longer have any 'meaning' (or have only a marginal value).

According to Baudrillard, the strategy of the present system is the maximizing of the word and the over-production of meanings. The 'system' demands us to form and free ourselves as subjects, to vote, to produce critical speech, and to act as active individuals in the media-festival of participation. Deviation and critical theory and politics are not objects for repression and oppression. They are coded in society on the basis of the functional definitions of demands. Even the last offender is defined by a social and rational relation. Criticism is the last argument for the existence of social space, use of power, the system of politics of differences (Baudrillard 1983b).

A way for a strategic 'resistance' in this situation is to deny the production of meanings and words. Strategic resistance of object and mass is not to participate and not to produce re-legitimation of the system; it refuses to absorb meanings for itself, and like a mirror, it reflects all the attempts to manipulate it back to the sender. Instead of this, according to Baudrillard, all the movements with confidence in emancipation (in abolition) do not see that they are co-operating with the system. They only renew the simulation of the ruling.

A 'Third' Phase: The Politics of Undecidability

What is the strategic meaning of the critical legal theory (abolition) in the Baudrillardian challenge: has its meaning disappeared, has it any longer some other function than to act as a pre-coded criticism of the official control system?

Perhaps it would be "reasonable" to read again some abolitionist texts (both theoretical and practical) with their manifold conflicts and contradictions. In these deconstructive readings and re-readings, one can find 'traces' or 'breaks' in abolition which resist being 'defined.' Through these readings, one may find more radical ways to interpret and 'act' in post-modern condition than criticism, which is still stuck in Truths and Utopias.

These post-legal-philosophical strategies should open their discourse and writing to the post-modern condition. Instead of building/re-building legitimation mechanisms of the law; or instead of looking for referents of the law; or instead of 'correcting/changing' the legal system towards more discursive and rational practices, a post-modern jurisprudence should challenge the whole idea and mirage of the law and the legal way of thinking. At the same time it would break the myth of the democracy and rationality of the law. To 'do' this it 'must' re-read political and social practices in the post-modern more 'radically' than before by opening its reading to the laws of the text and to the genetic and statistical codings of 'social' activities. The hu-Man is no more a citizen (a subject, a male), but a consumer (an object, a female), but the legal theory still analyzes the world of the male social contract by citizens and subjects. The strategy for post-... is the strategy of objects, consumers and females.

The third generation of abolition has three kinds of 'functions' when it moves between strategies of decriminalization and deconstruction:

1 It should deconstruct the (criminal) law at the level of legal norms, at the level of system building discourses, i.e. legal theory, jurisprudence and at the level of the methodology of law, i.e. the texts that are taken for granted, the ideas that justify different power structures, read the antinomies of the law.

2 It should deconstruct the story/stories of critical jurisprudence, particularly at the level of the general and abolition.

3 It should re-read the texts of the mechanisms of the law and social control in post-modern times.

Perhaps from texts of abolition, one could find a challenge to the post-modern information (control) factories. Perhaps abolition could be a refusal to produce information and signs for controlling political discourse (without modernism's moral and political utopias), criticism which is not as much pre-coded to the system as that of modern abolition.

It would not be reformist where the 'critic remains in the sphere of the criticized, he belongs to it, he goes beyond one term of the position but does not alter the positions of the terms' (Lyotard 1984). Because post-abolitionism has no transcendental and transhistorical evaluative term, it has to recognize its own conditions of existence, re-read and re-read again its 'strategies.' Maybe from this position a post-politics is possible, which is politics of irony and play, and which no longer takes the system seriously.

This irony means a challenge to political power and to 'critical' theory and practices (as abolition) which

> have endeavored to camouflage this fundamental challenge in the form of force relations such as dominator/dominated and exploiter/exploited, thereby channeling all resistance into a frontal relation (even reduced to microstrategies, this conception still dominates in Foucault: the puzzle of guerrilla warfare has simply been substituted for the chessboard of classical battle.) For in terms of force relations, power always wins, even if it changes hands as revolutions come and go. (Baudrillard 1987: 53).

Maybe the idea of 'difference' and appreciation of conflicts are precursors of something radical, something that does not only work for 'emancipation' of logos and phallos, but also asks who and how the idea of a self-knowing subject is coded, who speaks in us and who speaks for us. Maybe abolition could then be a textual/political strategy moving between different strategies of the other. Instead of a determined position, it could move from politics to texts, from deconstruction to destruction, from feminism to abolition. This non-essentialism and this politics of undecidability will not find rest from the universal moral values and principles (the Law of Emancipation, Freedom and Equality). Instead it is an unfinished movement, unfinished textuality, which is based on ...?

Postmodern abolition becomes the 'unfinished' and undecidable when it is all the time escaping and seducing conventional wisdom, the force of institutions, the walls of prisons, of the body/gender/genre, and when it has no Post (radical or reformistic). It is not based on any universal moral theory or universal moral values and principles (which are usually values and principles, that are based on ideological constructions as structures written by white, European males). Postmodern abolition is not based on essentialism: it has no assumptions about the nature of the woman and the man, or about the true nature of human beings or the just society). There is no morality (*Moralität* in the sense of Immanuel Kant). Instead we should speak about situationalism and ethics or situations. In different contexts ethics get different interpretations, different meanings, and different readings. This kind of ethics is not based on the universal Law (*lex aeterna, lex divina,* or *lex naturalis*) or on the Law of the Father. Maybe, and perhaps, it is instead 'based' on a justice or on ethics of justice, which is not about human rights or individual rights, but about inter-subjectivity, about otherness, and about relationships. The only ethics is ethics of the other. The postmodern abolitional style is irony, parody, and play, and its Utopia has burst and vanished in the thin air of the post-modern.

The Morality and The Utopia are imploded and The Truths are indefinitely unfinished. In the postmodern, there is no possibility of deciding where the border-line goes in dichotomies like good/bad, man/woman, rationality/irrationality, reality/representation, political activity/theoretical activity, active/passive, etc. We cannot get totally away from the tradition of the modern enlightenment and its dichotomous and moralist way of thinking, because we carry it in us and in our language. But we should challenge it anyway by asking whose morality, which rationality? American legal philosopher Drucilla Cornell (1990: 686) has an 'answer': reality ' ... is seen and constructed through the male gaze.' And maybe this is also the reality of abolition (or Eurocentric abolition): Radical strategies in this reality are non-essentialist feminism, which according to Cornell (1990: 687):

> feminism must seek truth-value, ... in the allegories and myths of the feminine. Feminism is always modified differently as different groups of women insist on their reality. As I have argued, being cannot be separated from seeing, but it cannot be reduced to it either. Indeed, it is precisely because of the impossibility of this separation that what 'is' cannot be reduced to the way one particular group sees reality. Other visions are always possible. There is always the possibility of slippage between what is seen and what 'is,' even if we can only understand the significance of the slippage from another point of view.

This is, or can be, or maybe is also, the radical strategy of post modern anti-reductionist abolition. But what about undecidable?

The undecidable is a term used by philosopher Jacques Derrida. He does not believe that today there is any question of choosing. Derrida (1973: 128) writes:

> There is, then, probably no choice to be made between two lines of thought; our task is rather to reflect on the circularity which makes the one pass into the other indefinitely. And, by strictly repeating this circle in its own historical possibility, we allow the production of some elliptical change of site, within the difference involved in repetition; this displacement is no doubt deficient, but with a deficiency that is not yet, or is already no longer, absence, negativity, nonbeing, lack, silence.

And this is also what my text tries to do (or is a starting point for a 'project,' for a politics not of the unfinished but of undecidability). By going through the narratives of modern philosophy as politics of emancipation (abolition is only one version and one genre), by going through it with undecidable's logic, by going and going ... by going and reading these circles of abolitionist movements 'some elliptical change of site' (ibid.) may be happening. I am not choosing between moralism and ideologism, or between them and postmodernism, but instead reading all these different traits, all these different signifiers, all these different texts. The third position of abolition is nothing more than one circle, which should also be decentered, deconstructed, and re-read. Abolition is undecidability. Theoretical abolition is deconstruction in the sense that "'To deconstruct' philosophy would ... be to think the structured genealogy of concepts in the most faithful or interior manner...' (Derrida 1972: 13).

The politics on abolitionism as a politics of undecidability has intercourse with French feminist writer and philosopher Helene Cixous' (1976) 'post'-feminism when she declares its 'position':

> If she's a her-she, it's in order to smash everything, to shatter the framework of institutions, to blow up the law, to break up the 'truth' with laughter

And maybe the ideology of the western hu-man-ism (and the abolition) is also an institution, a Law, which should be shattered, which should be blown up and from which we should try to move away by asking: who is the one who speaks in me, who is the one who speaks in me? This is why I also try to deconstruct the different phases or abolition by misreading them.

REFERENCES

Baudrillard, Jean. 1983a. *Simulations*. New York: Semiotext(e)

– 1983b. *In the Shadows of the Silent Majorities*. New York: Semiotext(e)

– 1987. *Forget Foucault*. New York: Semiotext(e)

Cixous, Helene. 1976. 'The Laugh of Medusa: A Manifesto for Women's Writing.' *Signs*, 1 (1): 875-893

Christie, Nils. 1981. *Limits to Pain*. Oxford: Martin Robertson

Cohen, Stanley. 1987. *Folk Devils and Moral Panics; The Creation of the Mods and Rockers*. New York: St. Martins

Cornell, Drucilla. 1990. 'The Doubly-Prized World: Myth, Allegory and the Feminine.' *Cornell Law Review*, 75 (3): 644-699.

Dalton, Clare. 1988. 'An Essay in the Deconstruction of Contract Doctrine,' in S. Levinson and S. Mailloux, eds., *Interpreting Law and Literature. A Hermeneutic Reader*. Evanston, IL: Northwestern University Press

Daudi, Philippe. 1988. *In (Re)-Search of Plentitude; Some Epistemological Remarks in the Postmodern Era*. Paper prepared for the Language and Politics Colloquium, University of Helsinki

Derrida, Jacques. 1986. 'But, Beyond ...' *Critical Inquiry* 13 (Autumn): 155-170

– 1977. 'Signature Event Context.' *Glyph*, 1: 172-197

– 1973. *Speech and Phenomena and Other Essays on Husserl's Theory of Signs*. Evanston, IL: Northwestern University Press

– 1972. *Positions*. Paris: *Editions de Minui*t

Foucault, Michel. 1977a. *Discipline and Punish*. London: Pantheon

– 1977b. *Language, Counter-Memory, Practice. Selected Essays and Interviews*, D.F. Bouchard, ed. Ithaca, NY: Cornell University Press

Gallop, Jean. 1985. *Reading Lacan*. Ithaca, NY: Cornell University Press

Hulsman, L., and B. J. de Celis. 1982. *Peines Perdues; Le Systeme Penal en Question*. Paris

Kristeva, Julia. 1986. 'Women's Time,' in *The Kristeva Reader*, 187-213. New York: Columbia University Press

Lacan, Jacques. 1977. 'The Mirror Stage as Formative of the Function of the I as Revealed in Psychoanalytic Experience,' in Jacques Lacan, *Ecrits*. New York/London: Norton/Tavistock

Lyotard, Jean-Francois. 1984. *The Post-Modern Condition*. Minneapolis: University of Minnesota Press

De Man, Paul. 1979. *Allegories of Reading*. New Haven, CT: Yale University Press

Mathiesen, Thomas. 1974. *The Politics of Abolition*. Oslo: Oslo University Press

Olsen, Frances. 1990. 'Feminism and Critical Legal Theory: An American Perspective.' *International Journal of the Sociology of Law*, 18 (2): 199-215

Vattimo, Gianni. 1987. "Verwindung: Nihilism and the Post-Modern Philosophy." *Substance*, 53: 7-17

8   Where Should the Movement Move?

Frank M. Dunbaugh

Good morning, I am an Abolitionist. Thank you for this opportunity to discuss the abolition movement with all of you distinguished advocates. This week I will facilitate sessions which our program calls 'Addressing Legislators Internationally.' In planning your time, please note that these are discussion sessions, not panels of people telling you what they know.

In my view, it is time to get down to the nitty gritty of abolishing the entire penal law system. Until we are able to describe clearly our vision of life without a punitive system, we cannot begin to develop a strategy for getting there. I hope that at this, our fifth conference, we will begin to work out some techniques and strategies. In establishing our expectations for ICOPA 5, it may be useful to look back at our previous conferences and what we sought to achieve at each of them.

The ICOPA Experience

ICOPA I at Toronto, 1983. I was very honored to be allowed to make one of the keynote addresses at Toronto. At that time, the movement was very frail. I was acutely aware that the crusaders in the US movement for a Moratorium on Prison Construction had not met for about four years, and that nothing was then planned. We had gotten our juices flowing in Kansas City in 1979, but there had been no follow-up. In Kansas City, we had been unable to agree on supporting the abolition of prisons, but we came close with a statement put out under the name of the National Alliance to Reduce Imprisonment.

The first ICOPA at Toronto had a good turnout and lots of enthusiasm, but it was short on funds for future organization, so I worried that we would never see one another ICOPA conference. My only real goal in Toronto was to ensure that there would be a second ICOPA. It is good that so many of the people who were in Toronto are here for our fifth conference at Indiana University today.

ICOPA II at Amsterdam, 1985. This was a wonderful conference. Herman Bianchi, Rene van Swaaningen and the Free University were marvelous hosts, and we had excellent facilities. For Amsterdam, I wrote a paper on strategies for abolishing prisons in the United States, but the conference taught me that we should reach further. My paper was premature, because I did not have a good concept of where prison abolition should lead us.

At ICOPA II, the movement made a great advance – from prison abolition to penal abolition – a change in language which was *intended* to broaden our objective. The Dutch sponsors of ICOPA II presented it as a subtle change in the title of the event, but as the conference developed, it became obvious that abolition of the entire penal law system had to become our goal. A highlight of ICOPA II was the representation from many European countries. Another feature was Kay Harris' paper (presented by Andy Hall) on the feminist perspective of crime and justice.[1] After Amsterdam, I hoped we would form an international network.

ICOPA III at Montreal, 1987. When no framework was developed to maintain and expand the international network of Abolitionists, my goal for Montreal was to create a stable abolitionist organization. Unfortunately, no permanent structure came from the Montreal meetings, a great disappointment. The only scheduled social session was at the opening of the conference. Thereafter, there were few structured opportunities to meet new people. Also, because there were virtually no plenary sessions after the opening, it was difficult to network or to plan for any continuation of the movement. The most important developments in Montreal were that Hal Pepinsky was able to steer the next conference to Poland, and Gordon Husk agreed to publish a newsletter. The few efforts to plan for the future all took place at informal private sessions not open to everyone. This appearance of elitism bruised the atmosphere at Montreal.

ICOPA IV at Warsaw, 1989. This conference was out of reach for me. I had planned to go, but other commitments and expenses barred my attendance. I am very sorry to have missed what everyone has described as a very successful conference. The presence of Bianchi, Christie, Hulsman, Mathiesen and Pepinsky, all at the same conference, was a unique achievement for Monika Platek and the other organizers. Happily, a report from ICOPA IV is available here.

ICOPA V at Bloomington, 1991. This looks like it will be a great conference. Certainly, the facilities are up to those we had at the Free University in Amsterdam. The program has been well planned to allow adequate opportunities to meet everyone in social as well as professional settings, and to meet in plenary sessions where we can plan to advance the movement toward the future.

Having this conference in Indiana has special meaning for me, because on my first trip to Indiana (about twenty years go), I became a prison abolitionist. At that time, I was a Deputy Assistant Attorney General for Civil Rights in the US Department of Justice. Some of our lawyers were considering instituting a suit against the State of Indiana to enjoin the state corrections officials from inflicting cruel and unusual punishment on the state's prisoners by housing them in overcrowded, inhumane conditions. When I came with them to inspect the prison at Michigan City, it was the first time I had ever seen a large warehouse with a five-story cage inside. My immediate reaction was that no human being should be in such a place for any length of time, no matter when they did. I now know that there are many such institutions. As we moved on to visit the Pendleton 'Reformatory' and the women's 'cottages' just outside Indianapolis, I realized that cages can take many forms, but, in whatever form it takes, imprisonment is cruel *per se.*

Goals for ICOPA V

With respect to this conference, it is my concern that we Abolitionists must progress with our dialogue. There has been a tendency for us to keep saying the same things to one another. Because we reach out to bring new people into the movement, we continually reiterate the justifications for our abolition posture. I, for one, do not need further persuasion to cast off the criminal law system. I am ready for a serious discussion about how that may be accomplished. Hopefully, the sessions assigned to me will become the forum for such discussions. In addition, we have a substantial need for mechanisms that will enable us to continue the dialogue during the intervals *between* ICOPAs. It would be a shame for us to recess our discussions for a two-year hiatus when we leave Indiana on Saturday.

Accordingly, my goal for this conference is twofold. The first is to explore alternatives to the penal law system in the context of specific offenses and offense categories in order to begin devising concrete non-punitive means for securing the important communal interests sought to be protected by the criminal law. The second is to create an international network that can continue beyond ICOPA V to explore the alternatives to the penal law system and to be a vehicle by which we can help one another in our academic and advocacy pursuits.

My experience in law enforcement convinces me that a community's interest can be promoted without a punitive legal system. I spent twenty years (1958-78) in the US Department of Justice enforcing the federal civil rights laws. We learned early on that we could not achieve much by trying to prosecute local officials who denied to black citizens their constitutional rights. The burden of proof is too high in criminal cases,[2] and juries tend to reinforce local customs.[3] The *1957 Civil Rights Act* authorized the Attorney General to initiate *civil* suits to enforce voting rights. In this way, we could sue voter registrars in *non-jury cases* seeking court orders to require them to use the same standards for black applicants that they used for white applicants and to place qualified black persons on the official voter registration lists. No effort was made to blame these local officials or to prosecute them criminally, although it is a federal crime to intentionally deprive a citizen of a constitutionally protected right. The long struggle for civil relief achieved some very limited successes, but the slow progress eventually was used to justify enactment of the *1965 Voting Rights Act* that suspended the use of all literacy tests in States which had discriminated in voter registration.

Later civil rights laws authorized the Attorney General to bring civil suits to enjoin discriminatory practices in housing and employment; to desegregate schools, public facilities, and public accommodations; and to remedy unconstitutional conditions in state-run institutions.[4]

Extracting Legitimate Interests From the Penal Codes

In my mind, lawyers and law professors ('Advocates for Justice,' I call them) are needed in the abolition movement, because what we seek is basically a reform of the legal system. That is not to say that the alternatives we decide to pursue will necessarily be incorporated into the legal system, only that they will be designed to supplant a part of the present legal system. Since we are trying to replace the criminal law, we must look at the penal codes with a view to understanding their proper role in society. Few people will agree to the abolition of the penal law system simply because it is immoral, or even because it is ineffective, unless we can identify precisely what legitimate public interests the system is supposed to protect and offer a moral and effective way to implement those communal interests.

It is important to *refine* our discussions so as to focus on the *interests* that are to be protected. Are they *legitimate* community interests? Can they be protected without doing harm? As a preliminary matter, I have analyzed some standard criminal codes and texts. I am hopeful that we will have the opportunity this week to examine these codes and begin to develop a real understanding of what they were designed to do.

Blackstone's Commentaries. Just before the American Revolution, William Blackstone wrote an authoritative treatise on the then current English common law. As it turned out, *Blackstone's Commentaries* (Gavit 1941) have become the definitive work on what the common law was in America before the States became sovereign and could enact their own laws.[5] With respect to the criminal law, Blackstone described five major categories of crime, according to whose interests were to be protected. The categories are:

1 *Crimes against religion or the church*, which include: blasphemy, cursing, witchcraft and sorcery, lewdness, and drunkenness.

2 *Crimes against the law of nations*, which include: passport violations, offenses against ambassadors, and piracy.

3 *Crimes against the crown*, which include: treason, assaults in the court, embezzling public funds, misconduct in office, disobeying an order of the King, and speaking against the King's authority.

4 *Crimes against the state*, which include five subcategories:

   a offenses against public justice, such as bribery, perjury, and obstruction of justice, *b* offenses against the public peace, such as riotous assemblages, unlawful hunting, and spreading false news,

c offenses against public trade, such as smuggling, usury, and false bankruptcy,

d offenses against public health, such as evading quarantine, and selling unwholesome provisions, and

e offenses against public, police, or economy, such as clandestine marriages, bigamy and polygamy, vagrant soldiers and mariners, idleness, gypsies, nuisances, luxury and extravagance, and gambling.

5 *Crimes against private interests*, which include three subcategories:

a offenses against persons, such as murder, rape, assault, battery, and kidnapping,

b offenses against habitations, such as arson and burglary, and

c offenses against property, such as larceny, robbery, malicious mischief, and forgery.

Almost everything for which the public now demands law and order falls into the fifth category.[6] In the eighteenth century, as Blackstone said, offenses against individuals were crimes *only because communal interests were affected*, leaving some conflicts between individuals for private resolution.[7] This relatively new part of the criminal law was still growing in 1776. The ancient legal systems had no equivalent.[8] Roman law provided a forum for *citizens* to initiate suits for injuries caused by private wrongs. In early England, private disputes were settled locally, according to feudal tradition, by the lord of the manor. It was only as the English crown sought to expand its control (and fees), that the jurisdiction of the King's courts was increasingly extended to private disputes by expanding the concept of a breach of the King's peace (Pollack and Maitland 1898: 463). In those days, the victim had to hire a prosecutor, so that use of the penal law was usually controlled by wealthy victims, not by the state.

In modern times, however, as Roscoe Pound (1972: 5) observes, 'The state has achieved almost a complete monopoly of force as a regulative instrument.' Herman Bianchi (1988) says our mission is to break the state's monopoly on conflict resolution. The modern expansion of penal law is apparent from examining a recent United States text (Clark and Barnes 1967) on criminal law.[9] Like Blackstone, this text also lists five categories of crimes, but at least three are in Blackstone's last category, and the traditional government interests (like treason, bribery, and perjury) seem to have been dropped to last place. The modern categories are:

1 Offenses against persons.

2 Offenses involving sexual behavior, morality and family relations.

3 Offenses against property.

4 Offenses against homes.

5 Offenses affecting government.

The criminal and penal codes of other nations also categorize offenses according to the interests to be protected. They show some variations that may reflect differing national histories or priorities. The Canadian Criminal Code lists nine rather confused categories of crimes.[10] The Spanish Penal Code has a slightly different emphasis, reflecting some concern for individual rights, maybe because it was written to replace a dictatorial regime.[11] The Soviet Criminal Code reflects certain communist economic interests not included in the Western codes and also includes military crimes.[12] There is a need to make comparisons of penal codes from various cultures, in order to develop a greater appreciation and comprehension of the range of the protections sought to be achieved by these statutory schemes.

Our focus need not be directed to the prohibited actions defined in the codes as criminal behavior. We should concentrate on the danger perceived by the lawmakers as requiring the defense of the penal law. For example, the Maryland fraud statutes include many criminal provisions, such as making it a crime 1) to advertise unavailable merchandise to induce sales of other merchandise, 2) to use simulated court documents to induce payment of a claim, and 3) to fail or refuse to give the purchaser of purebred livestock a certificate as to breed.[13] Each of these crimes would seem to have been enacted to protect consumers, but since their existence is not well known, it is doubtful that they do so effectively. What these laws do is to simplify the proof for the prosecutor (if his case fits these special facts), because the statute spells out the offense with greater particularity than a general fraud statute would.[14] It would appear that a much wider and more effective protective net could be cast. Why not have the state sponsor a broad consumer education program *and* have the state employ readily available attorneys with special knowledge (real estate, antiques, livestock, grains, wholesale foods, etc.) to oversee any major sales, at the request of either the seller or the purchaser? This might eliminate some criminal cases and, perhaps, many civil cases as well.

The crimes of murder, mayhem, and battery all involve the infliction of bodily injury. What is the true purpose of the criminal statutes with respect to them? Obviously, *no ex post facto* prosecution provides the victim of the crime with any protection, and only the civil law is available to award damages for the injury. So, it must be said that these crimes were designed for another purpose – perhaps to reform the offender or to intimidate other potential offenders, as a means to protect other potential victims of similar crimes *which have not yet occurred.* If so, the most important alternatives to criminal prosecutions of this type may have nothing to do with the alleged offenders. To illustrate, if many assaults occur in the vicinity of a row of abandoned houses, the city should consider a program designed to ensure occupancy of the houses. If assaults occur in a particular dark, blind alley, installing lights and a closed circuit monitor might be much more effective, and less costly, than threats of prosecution. Devising effective means of reducing fearful incidents of bodily injury, may be the best alternative to the use of penal sanctions in cases of violence.

To the extent, however, that the danger generally perceived by the community is that the perpetrator of a violent attack on another person is likely to attack again, it is time that we, as a community, deal with those fears directly. One problem with the penal law is that it does *not* face the issue of preventive detention honestly. It purports to punish an offender for a discrete and amply probed *past act,* but the sentence, which is imposed as a punishment, often includes elements of deterrence (based on what someone else *might* do in the future) and incapacitation (based on what the offender *might* do in the future).[15] Yet no evidence is required nor are any findings made as to the likelihood of *future* unlawful behavior by the offender.[16]

Since the fact of an offender's future dangerousness is never litigated, it can not be appealed. Although many of us may feel it is immoral to authorize incapacitative detention,[17] a statutory mechanism for this purpose would at least require an evidentiary record, findings in the trial court, and an appeal on the basis of whether the proved material and relevant facts support a finding of future dangerousness. This might be better than the present system which allows long-term carceral sentences to be upheld simply as appropriate and within the limits of the Legislature's punitive guidelines.[18] Both the moral and strategic aspects should be debated by Abolitionists.

Public Safety and Restorative Justice

The advocates of *restorative justice* have no problem imagining a civil law remedy, or even an informal negotiated remedy, in most cases of theft or minor assaults. Yet, there may be a pattern of behavior developing on the part of an offender which, in the judgment of the guardians of community safety (the police or the prosecutor),[19] ought not to be ignored. Even if we give priority to the claims of the victim and insure that the victim is able to be restored *before* the community attempts to take action against the offender, the community may still have a legitimate interest in initiating some defensive action. One might argue that such actions should not be punitive, but that injunctive restraints might be appropriate.

For example, if a person's offensive behavior indicates that he or she suffers from an addiction or chemical imbalance, the community may perceive a need to *impose* treatment.[20] This suggestion raises the sensitive issue of whether a person has the right to refuse medical treatment. But suppose the community decided to impose skills training to make an offender self sufficient, so as to reduce his or her need to steal? Is this fundamentally different from medication or counseling therapy? Should a public agency be able to determine the need for training or treatment, to evaluate proposed treatment plans, and to order implementation? Should a civil court make such decisions or review the agency process? The right to refuse treatment in such contexts is another issue for Abolitionists to debate.

Three problems with the ideal of informal dispute resolution and reconciliation come to mind and should be studied and discussed within the abolitionist circle. They are: 1) that the parties may not always be able to negotiate from positions of equality, 2) that resources are needed to investigate and organize the facts to facilitate the decision-making process, and 3) that the offender may not always have the resources to make adequate restitution. Means must be devised to give weaker participants greater leverage.[21] Part of the solution may be to provide adequate free resources so that the facts are not exclusively available to those who can afford to hire their own lawyers, accountants, and investigators.[22] Restitution plans also are likely to need considerable financial help.[23]

The Roots of the Abolitionist Movement

We are not here to *start* a revolutionary movement. The idea of abolition is quite old. It is hard to believe that it has been a dozen years since Kay Harris and I (Harris and Dunbaugh 1979) wrote a law review article on the abolition of prisons. At that time, we relied heavily on Fay Honey Knopp's *Instead of Prison* (1976) and Gilbert Cantor (1976). Honey Knopp (1976) cites many historical references for abolishing prisons, including quotes from Jesus[24] and Clarence Darrow (1902). Cantor postulated that the entire criminal law system could be abolished, and it seems to me that his article might well serve as a starting point for our discussions here in the sessions on 'Addressing Legislators.'

In turn, Cantor's article referred to a 1973 symposium in the *Wayne Law Review* on 'Dismantling the Criminal Law System,' which was based on a 1972 conference at the University of Kentucky in Lexington – only about two hours drive from here. In the lead article, Professor Michael Bayles cites Karl Menninger (1968). So one can see that the movement's roots are old and deep.

Since I was already in Indiana last week for the annual Delegate Assembly of Offender Aid and Restoration, I arrived here in Bloomington a few days early for this conference. This gave me an opportunity to surrender to my addiction for used book stores. In a shop in downtown Bloomington, I found a real gem which had come from the library of Edwin H. Sutherland.[25]

My prize book (Margaret Wilson 1931), published just a year after my birth, is a brilliant advocacy for abolition of the penal system. Noting that: *We must remember that crime, as distinguished from wrong doing, is a fact manufactured entirely by law."* (ibid.: 39, emphasis added), Ms. Wilson advanced all of the present-day arguments and rationales. She anticipated by over 50 years much of Kay Harris' (1991) feminist perspective,[26] and relied on the religious roots of abolition, much the same as does Honey Knopp (1976).[27] Wilson's book, bearing the same title later used by Menninger (1968), is *The Crime of Punishment.* Considering how long ago it was written, it is extremely well documented and filled with marvelous quotable material.[28] Wilson described herself as a housewife with no interest in crime and punishment until her husband became the governor of an English prison. Then, applying common sense and refusing to accept that there was anything that she could not understand, she studied criminology and became convinced that there was no acceptable rationale for the punitive system.

> I kept on inquiring diligently, without ceasing, into the real reasons for shutting men inside prisons. And the shattering discovery was that there is no acceptable reason for shutting four-fifths of the present prisoners in prison – and none for letting the other fifth out. Not only is there no reason for doing it, but there is no excuse for doing it. I had supposed in my thoughtlessness that prisons exist because there are criminals. I began to see that there are criminals largely because there are prisons. I discovered, with acute pain, that I had discovered none of these facts. For a hundred years, in many unread volumes, men who knew what they were talking about have been trying to say to the world what I began to realize – that crime is largely the result of the presence of bad laws and the lack of good ones. (Wilson 1931: 15-16)

> [A]s I watched the proceedings of local courts, I began to see very clearly that while one must obey all law – as long as it exists – one can respect very little law indeed. I saw that laws are not holy things to be worshipped, but efforts of the human mind to be judged and weighed ... Integrity of the mind implies a refusal to admire or respect unworthy things, whatever priesthood exacts our admiration ... We obey the law, but we need respect very little of it. We must not worship any of it. It is not God. It has no sanctity ... Let the law repent its blasphemous claims to sanctity, let it throw away its pretentious crown, and get into overalls like any other servant and do its job for the community, and then we will honor it endlessly. (ibid.: 16-17)

Margaret Wilson understood that some people must be confined for public safety, but that imprisonment is cruel *per se*, and prison *reform* is not the goal. She states (ibid.: 313):

> In our generation it is not only futile, it is fatuous for any State to mention its humanity while it sends men to prison for a day

longer than they need for the public safety to be there. What men think about prisons is not what sort of a cage they are in, but that they are in a cage. It would be no more humane to imprison men for a long term in the White House than it is to imprison them for a long time in prison. Neither would it be any more humane. It betrays a low sort of intelligence to boast at any time of anything, but what shall we say of a state which boasts of the money she spends on prisons, of modern plumbing she puts in, of the wireless, the food and the recreation, the libraries, or any other luxury she provides for her prisoners, while she keeps them locked up for thirty years for crimes which other states punish with two years? A murderer might as well plead that he shot his victim with a silver bullet, or that he administered poison out of a Venetian glass goblet. It is fundamentally cruelty and torture needlessly to cage a man. The only decency to a man inhumanely imprisoned is *to let him out.*

Ms. Wilson not only preferred a restorative system to a punitive one, but she wrote that we must change laws so as to *prevent* crimes. She observed that counterfeiting was reduced by making money extremely difficult to copy, and that the record keeping laws helped prevent bigamy in France. She said (ibid.: 298):

In England there is nowadays a good deal of bigamy, because the laws of divorce are so devastating to the poor. In France, it is practically impossible to commit bigamy. A man can't be married without a birth certificate, upon which every marriage and every divorce is endorsed. One wonders how much forgery, stealing and burglary might be made impossible if the brain of a nation was turned towards devising ways of prevention. But there is no hope of the brain of any nation being brought to this problem, until the nation realizes how terrible is the alternative of punishment.

My 1985 paper for ICOPA II also suggested that, 'The immediate task for abolitionists and reformers is to educate the public to the need for a pro-active program of crime prevention, so that political pressure will begin to stimulate the thinking of professionals and academics' (Dunbaugh 1986).

Ms. Wilson concludes her wonderful book (1931: 330) with the following indictment of the punitive model:

How can a community hurt a criminal it has created, which it has borne as truly as a mother bears a child? Considering the history of our cruelty, it seems that what we need more than anything else is to cleanse our minds from the idea of judicially exacting suffering for wrongdoing, to realize that our habit of punishment is as great an evil as any crime.

Obviously, we are not the first to advocate for the abolition of the criminal law. Anthropological studies indicate that there was no punitive system within primitive cultures, because they needed one another for communal benefits, mainly for food acquisition and defense. There was no punishment for members of the tribe, even if they failed to perform up to the community's expectations. It was understood that everyone knew what was expected, and peer pressure usually brought conformity. Failures were not looked upon as offenses against the group.[29] If a member truly could not get along with the tribe, that person left the group or was banished. I suspect that, in practice, exiles often moved in with other related tribes.

In a 1915 treatise on the *Origin of Punishment*, Ellsworth Faris wisely noted:

> Our institutions are so complex and our tendency to idealize the existent is to inveterate that we are driven from one theory of punishment to another in the effort to justify what may, perhaps, have no real justification. (Kocourek and Wigmore 1915: 151)

Faris observed that to punish is to declare an enemy. War with an enemy is not like punishment. There is no effort to measure pain, to make it proportional to the offense. Rivals tend to fight a deadly struggle. As Margaret Wilson said (1931: 22), group defense permits no measured response, so that each member must say to outsiders, 'The things which belong to any one man of us are more valuable to me than your life, and if you steal from any of my group, I shall take your life, or part of it.'[30] Based on his studies of primitive people, Faris (1915) observed:

> There is an abundant reason for questioning whether any one inside the primitive group was ever punished, at least by those within his own tribe. In an instinctive way the members of the group are bound together and in the most homogeneous groups they do not punish each other. Present-day people of some uncivilized tribes do not punish their children.

Someone suggested that penal abolition could mean retaining the criminal law and abolishing the penalties. Perhaps it will always be appropriate to announce and demonstrate community standards, and a formal court proceeding for placing guilt may be an appropriate vehicle. My mind is not closed to examining any approach, but I tend to suspect measures that leave a prosecutor looking for someone to condemn.

We will hear a great deal more about restorative justice, both here at ICOPA V and elsewhere. It is the new catch phrase. It is a promising concept which we should nurture, but we do not yet know what it will become. Let us be on our guard. If we allow the government to retain its monopoly on dispute resolution, but in a new, more attractive, dress, it may become more difficult to wrest control from the politically powerful.

Thank you for your attention and welcome to Bloomington. I look forward to our discussions this week.

NOTES

1 Modified versions of this paper were later published. See Harris (1987, 1991).

2 In 1960, my first prosecution, we proved that prisoners had been chained naked to the bars of their cells, while their genitals were assaulted with a high pressure water hose. The case was dismissed after 8 weeks of testimony because we had not proved that the responsible guards could understand The Constitution well enough to form the required specific intent to deprive prisoners of their rights.

3 Massive racially motivated purges of Black voters from the voter rolls in Louisiana in 1956 did not move a grand jury in Monroe, LA to return an indictment. Nor was any indictment forthcoming from a grand jury in Mobile, ALA, when the sheriff's posse and state troopers tear gassed and assaulted peaceful demonstrators at the Edmund Pettus Bridge in Selma, ALA in March, 1965.

4 United States Code, Title 42, Sec. 1971a. (voting), Sec. 1997a. (institutions), Sec. 2000a-5. (public accommodations), Sec. 2000b. (public facilities), Sec. 2000c-6. (public education), Sec. 2000e-6. (employment), and Sec. 3613. (housing).

Sec. 2000c-6. was part of Title IV of the *Civil Rights Act* of 1964, that also provided two other non-punitive means for desegregating the schools: 10 technical assistance under Title IV to help school boards plan the process, and 2) a mechanism in Title VI for cutting off federal financial aid to racially-segregated school districts.

5 Maryland (where I practice law) adopted the common law as its base (*Maryland Declaration of Rights*, Art. 5.), and some of the common-law crimes are still not codified. See *Ireland* v *State*, 310 MD. 328, 529 A.2d 365 (1987).

6 Most white-collar crimes such as consumer fraud and environmental crimes are in the fourth category, while official misconduct, such as civil rights violations, were often not criminal, except that embezzlement of public funds constituted a crime against the *crown*.

7 At p 770 (Gavit 1941), Blackstone describes the fifth category as offenses which }derogate from those rights and duties, which are owing to particular individuals, in the preservation of which the community is interested. He later states that:

> If these injuries were confined to individuals, they would come under the head of private wrongs, for which a satisfaction would be due only to the party injured; but they are of a much more extended import, because their commission involves a violation of the laws of nature; because they almost always include a breach of the peace; and because by their example and evil tendency they endanger all civil society. Hence, in addition to satisfaction due in many cases to the individual by action for the private wrong, the offender is liable to public punishment for the crime.

This passage is interesting, because if we leave the laws of nature to self enforce, and if we reject punishing for deterrence, then we are left with only a breach of the King's peace as the justification for prosecuting offenses against individuals, including murder, rape, robbery, and burglary.

8 Herman Bianchi (1988: 1) writes that:

> In antiquity, in Greek, Hebrew, Roman, and Germanic law, state control took place only in case of evidently important political matters. In all other cases of crime the members of the community devised a legal system which allowed them to regulate the conflict themselves.

And Morley (1914: 41) observes that:

[The Romans] drew no clear line between public and private wrongs. Nearly all offenses, as is common in primitive society, were treated as private wrongs. Only to a limited extent had the idea of crime as an offense against the public dawned upon the roman mind.

9 A treatise is analyzed because in the United States, there is no national penal (or criminal) code that would be the equivalent of a European penal code. Each of the 5 0 states has its own criminal law(only some of which are codified), and the national (federal code) is limited to matters over which the federal government has jurisdiction.

10 The categories are: 1) Crimes against public order, 2) Crimes against the administration of law and justice, 3) Sexual offences, public morals, and disorderly conduct, 4) Disorderly houses, gaming and betting, 5) Offences against the person and reputation, 6) Offences against the rights of property, 7) Fraudulent transactions relating to contracts and trade, 8) Wilful and forbidden acts in respect of certain property, and 9) Offences relating to currency.

11 The categories are: 1) Crimes against the external security of the state, 2) Crimes against the internal security of the state (includes crimes against the exercise of individual rights), 3) Counterfeiting, 4) Crimes against the administration of justice, 5) Crimes of public officials in exercising their duties, 6) Crimes against persons, 7) Crimes against morals, 8) Crimes against honor, 9) Crimes against the status of persons, 10) Crimes against liberty and security, 11) Crimes against property.

12 There are twelve categories: 1) Crimes against the state, 2) Crimes against socialist ownership, 3) Crimes against life, health, freedom, and the dignity of the person, 4) Crimes against the political and labor rights of the citizen, 5) Crimes against personal ownership of citizens, 6) Economic crimes, 7) Official crimes, 8) Crimes against justice, 9) Crimes against the system of administration, 10) Crimes against public security, public order, and the health of the population, 11) Crimes constitution survival of local custom, and 12) Military Crimes (Berman 1972).

13 Annotated Code of Maryland, Article 27, Sec. 195 (d) (bait and switch), Sec. 199 (a) (false court documents), and Sec. 211 (livestock certificates).

14 One cannot help wondering whether such statutes were proposed to the Legislature after an unsuccessful prosecution in a case of the type described in the law.

15 The concepts of incapacitation and deterrence, as appropriate objectives of the criminal law, are widely accepted among experts who are not abolitionists.

16 The deterrent effect seems to be assumed, perhaps based on the theory that the Legislature made a presumptive finding. We know, however, that the Legislatures have not held hearings or made any serious findings about deterrence, either generally, or with respect to particular offenses.

17 If the purpose was to protect potential future victims from the current offender, we would confine and punish:

> persons who the government asserts may (we can not be sure) someday (we know not when) commit an act (we know not what) which somehow (we know not how) will endanger another person (we know not whom). Yet the fact finding process by which people are selected for such preventive confinement does not even purport to examine the when, what, how, and whom of the feared future offense ... [T]o subject persons to imprisonment for what we *guess* they might do in the future constitutes a gross denial of human rights. (Harris and Dunbaugh 1979: 445)

What about locking them up for what we guess *someone else* might do in the future?

18 If deterrence and incapacitation were separated out from punitive sentences (by authorizing civil commitments), could we persuade the public that punishment by long imprisonment is cruel? Could we require a different standard of treatment for civilly committed detainees who are not being punished? The Court is likely to hold follow its rationale in *Bell* v. *Wolfish*, 441 U.S. 520 (1979) to hold that persons lawfully confined are not entitled to any better treatment than convicts, except that they may not be punished.

19 A serious problem is the definition of community and the level of self determination involved in the selection of those who are authorized to act on behalf of the community.

20 I do not mean to suggest that the alternative to criminal law is mental health law. This has been the criticism leveled at Dr. Karl Menninger.

21 Community dispute resolution is not likely to replace the class action suit against corporate giants for protection against consumer fraud, product defects, and toxic assaults.

22 We might consider some form of periodic mandatory community service from all citizens as a mechanism for finding the necessary resources to provide a level playing field. If we allowed voluntary service as a set-off against taxes, the citizenry might be able to effect significant changes in budgetary priorities.

23 There may be ways to assist an offender to create a voluntary support base made up of family members, friends, and supportive organizations. A program of government guaranteed loans to such support groups would be helpful. By putting innocent volunteer supporters in financial jeopardy, there is an added incentive to keep the offender out of prison and in the work force.

24 In Luke 4, 16-30, Jesus says that the Lord sent him 'to proclaim release for prisoners.'

25 Sutherland, who distinguished himself with prolific contributions to the field of criminology, was Professor of Sociology at Indiana University here in Bloomington.

26 For example, Wilson (1931: 287) writes that

> The first step in women's quest of an alternative to punishment is to repent, deeply and thoroughly, of respect for the law. Women can perform one invaluable service to the nation by meeting, in their organizations, to consider the absurdities, the hypocrisies, the unfairness, the indecencies, the cruelties, the inadequateness of the laws of their state – all the time obeying to the letter these laws for which they are responsible until they can manage to change them. They ought conscientiously and continually to attend their local courts and discuss and criticize all the processes of the law ... They could read Wines, Lawes, Gillan, Sutherland, Osborne, Havelock Ellis, Parry, Cairns – for every reading and digestion of these books is a service to the States cursed by ignorant voters. Women's clubs might get lawyers to come and defend the law to them ... [to] explain to them what justice really is, the implications of its Roman and Pagan origin.

And later (ibid.: 290):

> One knows what the legal profession will answer any such reckless women. They will say that a little knowledge is not a dangerous thing to lawyers, and that women can't understand these matters; in fact that no one but a lawyer with years of training can appreciate the magnificence of the scheme of justice. Yet they will not agree, that as a wit says, the laws of England, or of the United States of America, tend to become an official secret. The question rises, if determined women by a thorough course of reading cannot understand these things, how are the men of the street, without any such conscientious endeavor, to obey laws which they have not a chance of understanding.

27 For example, Wilson (1931: 287-288) asks whether 'a crucifix, an innocent man on a cross, would not be a better symbol of the workings of Roman justice than a blindfolded goddess with scales. Or would Pilate washing his hands in an attempt to shift responsibility be a still more fit emblem?'

She suggests that women should discuss criminal law with their clergymen:

> Ask them if our faith or our courts are right. Ask them if they believe in the infliction of pain and death for the crimes of pain and death, because the ancient Jewish law permitted the taking of an eye for an eye, and a hand for a hand, and a life for a life ... Ask them if Jesus believed in an eye for an eye, a life for a life ... Let the women ask their spiritual advisors their option of the retributory theory of punishment – but let them not accept it without thought.

> Ask them why the word Justice is not mentioned in the teachings of Jesus, nor, indeed, in the *New Testament*. Ask them if the whole Roman and Jewish conception of the human infliction of pain for wrongdoing is not exactly what Jesus strove by his teachings to overthrow. Ask them if he ever approved of punishment inflicted by anyone but an infinitely loving God. (ibid.: 290-291)

28 She quotes J.A.R. Cairns as saying:

> Like most things purchased by the poor, even Justice is coarser in fiber and cheaper in quality ... It is fantastic nonsense to say

that the Law takes no cognizance of the status of its citizens; it is worse than nonsense, it is hypocrisy ... The poor ought not to be subjected to a state of affairs which would be intolerable to the wealthy. (ibid.: 289)

29 Does this suggest that we have expanded our 'community' too far? In smaller families, tribes, or communities, it is possible to foster a loving and non-judgmental relationship among the members. But unlike early England when the jurors were expected to know the people and the facts in advance of trial, we now insist on putting the fate of our youth in the hands of people selected *because they are strangers with no knowledge of the circumstances surrounding the event they are to judge.* It may be fair, but is it wise?

30 When policy makers declare a war on drugs, or tax evasion, or whatever, it connotes exile from the protection of the community and a fight to the death. In this milieu, there can be no effective invitation to treatment, and offers to reconcile are often predicated on ultimatums to surrender.

REFERENCES

Berman, H.J. 1972 *Soviet Criminal Law and Procedure.* Cambridge, MASS: Harvard University Press

Bianchi, H. 1988. 'Returning Conflict to the Community.' *Tsedeka Justice,* 1 (1): 1

Cantor, G.M. 1976. 'An End to Crime and Punishment.' *The Shingle,* May: 98-114

Clark, W.L., and M.Q. Barnes. 1967. *A Treatise on the Law of Crimes,* 7th ed. Munline, IL: Callaghan

Darrow, Clarence. 1902. An address to the prisoners of Cook County Jail, Chicago.

Dunbaugh, Frank M. 1986. 'A Strategy for Abolishing Prisons in the United States,' in H. Bianchi and R. van Swaanigen, eds., *Abolitionism: Toward a Non-Repressive Approach,* 178-185. Amsterdam: Free University Press

Gavit, B.C.. 1941. *Blackstone's Commentaries on the Law.* Washington, DC: Washington Law Book Company

Harris, M. Kay and Frank M. Dunbaugh. 1979. 'Premise for a Sensible Sentencing Debate: Giving up Imprisonment.' *Hofstra Law Review*, 7 (2): 417-456

Harris, M. Kay. 1991. 'Moving into the New Millennium: Toward a Feminist Vision of Justice,' in H. Pepinsky and R. Quinney, eds., *Criminology as Peacemaking*, 83-97. Bloomington: Indiana University Press

Honey Knopp, Fay. 1976. *Instead of Prisons: A Handbook for Abolitionists.* Syracuse, NY: Prison Education Research Foundation

Kocourek, A., and J.S. Wigmore. 1915. *Evolution of Laws: Primitive and Ancient Legal Institutions.* Boston: Little Brown

Menninger, K. 1968. *The Crime of Punishment.* New York: Viking Press

Morley, W.G. 1914. *Outlines of Roman Law*, 2nd ed. New York: G.P. Putnam's Sons

Pollack, Sir F., and F.W. Maitland. 1978. *History of English Law*, 2nd ed. Cambridge: Cambridge University Press

Pound, R. 1972. *Criminal Justice in America.* New York: Da Capo Press

Wilson, M. 193 1. *The Crime of Punishment.* London: J. Cape